Writing Women

Contemporary Women Novelists

Olga Kenyon

PLUTO PRESS

London • Concord, Mass

First published in 1991 by Pluto Press
345 Archway Road, London N6 5AA
and 141 Old Bedford Road,
Concord, MA 01742, USA

British Library Cataloguing in Publication Data
Kenyon, Olga
    Writing Women.
    1.   Literature. Women writers. critical studies
    I.   Title
    809'.89287

ISBN 0–7453–0307–2

Library of Congress Cataloging in Publication Data
Kenyon, Olga.
        Writing women: contemporary women novelists/Olga Kenyon.
            p.   cm.
        Includes bibliographical references and index.
        ISBN 0–7453–0307–2
        1. English fiction–Women authors–History and criticism.
    2. English fiction–20th century–History and criticism.
    3. American fiction–Women authors–History and criticism.
    4. American fiction–20th century–History and criticism.
    5. Feminism and literature–History–20th century. 6. Women and
    literature–History–20th century. I. Title.
    PR888.W6K44 1990
    823'.9109287–dc20   90–47881
                                                                  CIP

ISBN 0–7453–0307–2

Typeset by Stanford Desktop Publishing Services, Milton Keynes
Printed and bound in the UK by Billing and Sons Ltd, Worcester

Writing Women

Contents

1   A Guide to Feminist Literary Criticism   1

2   Angela Carter: Fantasist and Feminist   12

3   Wandor, Rubens, Feinstein: 32
    Jewish Women Writing in Britain

4   Black Women Novelists: An Introduction   51

5   Alice Walker: The Colour is Purple   61

6   Toni Morrison: The Great American   83
    Novelist is a Black Woman

7   Caribbean Women Writers   99

8   Buchi Emecheta and Black Immigrant   113
    Experience in Britain

Useful Terminology   134
Bibliography   138
Index   148

To all those friends who have generously
helped with the re-reading
and re-writing of this book.

1
A Guide to Feminist Literary Criticism

In the last twenty years many of our institutions have felt the impact of the feminist revolution. Women are increasingly establishing themselves in previously male-dominated domains, from the media to the law, from the Church to business. The rising prominence of women's publishing is one such notable success, and has been crucial in the promotion of women's writing.

The study of history has begun to include women's history (*her*story), a discipline which strives to uncover women's lives and achievements, to acknowledge the contributions of women as scholars, researchers and writers. Every historical period and literary genre is undergoing reassessment from a feminist perspective: from life in the Middle Ages to contemporary science fiction; from modern media images to romantic fiction. Since the late 1960s, literary criticism has also broadened to include both readers and writers who are no longer presumed to be male, or white, or middle-class.

Within a patriarchal (that is, male-dominated) system, women have a different relationship to language than men. Women have been marginalised or stereotyped in everyday language, in literature and in society. Language has downgraded women in two obvious ways: by omission, as in the use of the word 'mankind' to denote *all* humans; and through pejorative words, such as 'cow', 'bird', 'skirt'. Language reveals the unequal value of gender: 'master' denotes dominance, whereas 'mistress' suggests belonging to a man. Literature is guilty of presenting us with stereotypes and male fantasies of women's behaviour: the long-suffering Griselda, the ever-patient Penelope, the vengeful Lady Macbeth, the scheming Becky Sharp.

Literary criticism has marginalised women by overlooking many women writers, from the Restoration writer Aphra Behn, to the 'romantic' Jean Rhys. Women have been excluded from leading posts in university English departments, and from most review-writing until recently. Even today women are the authors of only one-fifth of books published. Women novelists may still find themselves disparaged as such, in the same manner as 'lady novelists' were sneeringly referred to in the nineteenth century.

Feminists, who value women's experiences and potential, have re-read 'women's novels' with new eyes and have found a wealth of psychological, social and political insight. Dale Spender, in *Mothers of the Novel* (1987), has resuscitated a hundred neglected women novelists writing before Jane Austen. These women, Spender claims, created this 'new' form, and 'mothered' the novel. Gothic novels, for example, were pioneered by women such as Mrs Radcliffe in her popular novel *The Mysteries of Udolpho* (1794), extended by the Brontës and continued in this century by Iris Murdoch, Angela Carter and others, to express both the restrictions and fears still experienced by women, and their love of story-telling.

From Literary Theory to Feminist Literary Theory

If literature is the depiction of relations between the inner and outer selves, and between individuals and society, then literary criticism is the attempt to analyse these relationships in terms of language. In the past 25 years, the strongest influence in literary theory has been structuralism.

Previously, literary criticism acknowledged the writings of predominantly white, male British writers, such as Coleridge and Arnold, sanctified in Leavis's preaching of *The Great Tradition* in Cambridge in the 1940s.[1] Women writers and those from colonial and Third World cultures were ignored. Then new theories, many emanating from the linguist Saussure, rejected Leavis's school of criticism as 'humanist' and dismissed his anthropocentric view of the world.[2] Before Saussure, meaning was thought to exist in the mind or in the object. Saussure claimed that meaning lay in language, in the relations between its parts, its *structures*. Structuralism's arguments unsettlingly assert that there is no neutral, or objective ground for criticism and meaning. Saussure's revolutionary insight is that meaning does not precede language, but is constructed in it. Language is both a social product of the faculty of speech, and a collection of necessary conventions. Meaning is not intuitive, but learned, and differs from language to language.

All attributed meanings, all judgements, mask our underlying ideology, that is, our moral, psychological and political presuppositions about the world. Questioning a presupposed ideology is a rewarding approach for women since the process reveals so many implicit assumptions about such concepts as 'maternal instincts', 'women's intuition' and others. New theories invite us to examine the assumptions which underpin our notions of reading and attributing meaning – both far more complex and problematical than previously presumed.

The influences of structuralism are embodied in one of the primary principles of feminist literary criticism: that no account, no theory is ever completely impartial or neutral. This concept gives validity to the subjective experience of the reader. Politically, feminist literary criticism aims to expose, not perpetuate, patriarchal practices and attitudes. It questions patriarchal, 'universal' definitions of what constitutes knowledge, in order to open up social, political and cultural systems to the vast majority of women *and* men who are not in positions of power.

This widespread questioning of power originated with Freud, Marx, and Saussure. Freud dethroned the concept of the monolithic human personality, while his findings on psychosocial development shattered many ideas on sexuality. Marx made economics central to a definition of society, while Saussure questioned basic assumptions about meaning in language. We are in the exciting process of redefining human nature and reality, and the influence of language on our sexual development, politics, and literature.

Three Facets of Feminist Literary Criticism

Feminist critics claim that the *difference* between the sexes is so fundamental that it is an organising category of experience. They maintain that the inequality of the sexes is not biological but cultural, as suggested by many women's novels from *Jane Eyre* to *The Color Purple*. Feminist thought and women's writing have often cross-pollinated one another, as feminists found proof of their theories in literature, and as women became more experimental and politicised in their writings.

The last 15 years have seen an immense amount of work reflecting on the relation of women to writing, focusing on both a reassessment of women writers of the past, and the development of new forms of creative literature and critical studies. Within this developing canon of work, these critical studies divide roughly into three categories: one which uses women's *experience* as a critical determinant, another attempting to emphasise the political aspects of feminism, and finally one which explores women's relationship with language and psychoanalysis. However, these are very general divisions, and there is a great deal of overlap.

The American Approach: The 'Image of Women'

American women academics began in the 1960s to study the stereotyped characterisation of women in men's writing. They also analysed the patriarchal mechanisms which prevented women from writing, or, if they succeeded in writing, from being accepted into the literary canon. In 1970 Kate Millett produced a fierce attack on the male literary bastions in *Sexual Politics*. D.H. Lawrence, Henry Miller, Ernest Hemingway and others had been heralded as great writers and original thinkers on sexual morality; Millett, from a feminist perspective, exposed their portrayals of women as fantasy figures of wish-fulfilment and pornography, and their male characters' relationships with women as sado-masochistic. *Sexual Politics* was only one of the many books and articles that offered a critique of male-dominated literature and which challenged established (male) notions about how women are supposed to think, feel and react.

In the first wave of feminist literary criticism in the 1970s, Professor Elaine Showalter initiated the quest for a specifically feminine tradition in literary history. Showalter, Ellen Moers and Patricia Meyer Spacks take images of women in nineteenth-century novels and show the implicit criticism of society's treatment of women. In *A Literature of Their Own* (1978) Showalter provides a strong infrastructure with the concepts of sisterhood and women's culture as the basis for feminist criticism. She rejects typecast notions about female 'passivity' and 'hysteria' while revaluing the symbolic message in the heroines' adventures and the political implications in plots dismissed as 'contrived'.

At the beginning of her career, Ellen Moers investigated the problematic topic of 'feminine' metaphors in nineteenth-century fiction. In *Literary Women* (1977), she argued that metaphors of small birds, frightened animals, tiny stones etc. recur to symbolise women's perceptions of themselves. Such a view is debatable, but Moers' evolution as a critic is representative of many feminists over the past three decades. Like many reformist feminists, she was against the segregation of women from the mainstream, as Doris Lessing is, but by the 1960s she accepted the political necessity of viewing women as a distinctive group. By the time she published *Literary Women* Moers saw women's writing as a rapid and powerful undercurrent and insisted that one must know the history of women to understand the history of literature.

Patricia Meyer Spacks, concentrating on sexuality in personal life, explored adolescent development, self-perception, passivity and independence through discussion with her students. The result was *The Female Imagination* (1977) which concluded that it is possible to make some generalisations about women's attitudes and creativity 'that persist despite social change'. However, her study is flawed because her focus is limited to her (predominantly) white, middle-class students, and nineteenth-century, white middle-class novelists. More sensitive to issues of class and race is Annis Pratt in her work *Archetypal Patterns in Women's Fiction* (1981). She examines archetypes and similarities 'in the widest possible range' of novels, including political ideologies and lesbian experience.

American feminists use women's experience literally in their criticism reading for images of women. They see reading as communication between the life of the writer and the life of the reader. This can be an exhilarating experience, but it is inadequate for an analysis of language, or of blind spots. As a critic one cannot even grasp one's own position fully, therefore a reading which allows for 'omissions' is needed to complement the stress on authenticity. ('Omissions' could be Murdoch's omission of much of female experience, or Emecheta's omission of a wider critique of the social oppression of African mothers.)

The inherent weakness in the American 'images of women' critical approach is that it postulates too close a link between fiction and autobiography. Marxist and socialist feminists criticise this approach as unoriginal in its actual reading of a literary text. They reject the belief that texts fully express experience, and that the more 'authentic' the experience, the more valuable the text will be. Many of those who work with the Marxist/socialist perspective are from Britain.

Political Feminist Criticism in Britain

Britain has produced a wide selection of bold young feminist critics. Many combine socialist or Marxist theoretical interest in the production and ideology of literature with an emphasis on women's experience. Mary Jacobus, Rosalind Coward, Michele Barrett and Cora Kaplan all foreground feminist concerns for women's writing, within a political framework. Topics which socialist feminists discuss include domestic labour, the effects of class discrimination and low pay, women's position in the family and the labour force – concerns in many novels of the 1970s and 80s. Radical feminists work in woman-only political groups, but agree with their socialist sisters that gender is not biologically but culturally determined.

Some younger feminists agree with older women writers in rejecting an essential difference between male and female. They emphasise that politics based on this idea risk inverting the old, hierarchical distinction between male and female, leaving the distinction itself firmly entrenched. Iris Murdoch and Alison Lurie are among those who refuse to be ghettoised, arguing that sexual difference is a matter of biological fact which does not prevent their sharing 'male' language and political and literary preoccupations.

In resisting accepted readings of literature, socialist feminists' criticism extends *beyond* the book to the culture which has coerced women into contradictory or marginalised positions. They highlight the effects of capitalism on a writer's outlook and the effects of economic production on book distribution. They look at the role and wording of mass media and advertisements, to see where and how women are placed in limiting, invidious roles, such as the nagging spouse, the happy housewife, the harassed working 'Supermum'. In these examinations, these feminist critics resemble the French structuralists, since everyday examples are as illuminating to analyse as 'high' literature.

When the rigid distinctions between high and low culture are diminished, questions on the differences between feminist fiction and women's fiction emerge. Angela Carter is an adventurous creator of fictions, drawing on women writers of the past and playing with romantic and stereotypical female characters. These romantic characters are not necessarily feminist in themselves, but when treated critically and openly, they reveal the social construction of consciousness, ideology and imagery. Women's fiction, as opposed to feminist fiction, only reveals this construction *implicitly*.

French Feminists and the Concept of *Difference*

French feminist critics use the work of the neo-Freudian psychoanalyst Jacques Lacan to examine how the 'feminine' has been defined, represented or repressed. They examine the symbolic systems of language, philosophy, psychoanalysis and art, and have produced a body of imaginative theoretical work. They proclaim the death of patriarchy and of the privileged work of art; their reading of texts is subversive and political.[3]

For French (and many younger British) feminist critics the concept of *difference* is essential. Psychoanalysis posits a difference between the constitution of feminine and masculine subjects. Lacan claimed that this difference is constituted as an effect of the acquisition of language. Theoretically, this would lead to a difference in the relationship of men and women to language.

The adventurous writers Luce Irigaray and Hélène Cixous explore the question of how far women's writing differs from men's.[4] They consider that language patterns may be influenced by deep libidinal energies. Libidinal drives which can find no place in the regimented discourse of patriarchal reason suffuse female writings. Men may gain access to such writing, and may occasionally produce it. The example often used is Molly Bloom's long soliloquy in Joyce's *Ulysses*.

Some English feminists endorse these ideas, first explored by Virginia Woolf. She, like Irigaray and Cixous, glimpsed a 'woman's sentence' in occasional, fragmentary forms. This mode of writing holds the promise of deliverance from male habits of thought. The characters in her fiction, and that of French novelist Nathalie Sarraulte, support this idea: many of the male characters are trapped in repressive 'rational' ways of thinking, while the women display greater powers of intuition.

Julia Kristeva extends Lacan's distinction between an imaginary and a symbolic order. Briefly the symbolic order accepts the phallus as the representation of the Law of the Father, which dominates human society. The imaginary order is that of the mother; Kristeva calls this order the 'semiotic', linked to oral and anal drives which flow across the child. Some discourses, like art, poetry and madness, draw on the semiotic rather than the symbolic aspects of language. The semiotic pervades modernist poetry, and the novels of Virginia Woolf with their apparent lack of logical structure, in which the rhythms of the body and the unconscious break through conventional social meaning.

Interestingly, Kristeva argues that it is not woman but motherhood which has been repressed and instead of our present emphasis on gender we should analyse many different discourses, in speech and in writing. Women's strategy must be to 'reject everything finite, definite, structured, loaded with meaning, in the existing state of society. Such an attitude puts women on the side of the explosion of social codes: with revolutionary movements.'[5]

From *Difference* to *Deconstruction*

With his theory of *deconstruction*, Jacques Derrida challenges the foundation of Western thought on metaphysics, that is, any system of thought which claims an unassailable first principle. First principles, he believes, are commonly defined by what they exclude, and stem from polar oppositions: male/female, active/passive, mind/ body, good/evil. In male-dominated societies, man is the founding principle and woman the excluded opposite. His critical method, which he has called 'a strategy within philosophy', aims to *deconstruct* these binary opposites.

Kristeva is the French feminist most interested in literary criticism, and in structural aspects of the text. She wishes to undo – to deconstruct – the old barriers between linguistics and poetics (literary criticism) in order to construct a new science of *semiotics* or textual theory. The oppressive symbolic (male) order should be undermined by the semiotic – 'the pattern or play of forces we can detect inside language'. Though she considers the semiotic closely connected with 'femininity', it is not exclusive to women. Kristeva is wary of definitions and sees femininity as what is marginal, subversive, different. Femininity and womanhood are *not* the same but patriarchy makes them appear identical. So women come to represent the boundary between symbolic order and imaginary chaos, either virgin or whore, idealised or vilified.

Both Derrida and Kristeva attack the rigid boundaries between the accepted and the unaccepted. They wish to examine certain basic texts in order to *release* their multiplicity of possible meanings. In this way hierarchies are breached and undermined, but within the terms of the texts' own structures. Kristeva maintains that all meaning is contextual and that the most constructive criticism examines the whole text, including its ideological, social and psychoanalytical implications. She coined the useful concept of 'intertextuality' to indicate the necessity of acknowledging the influence of other texts. Kristeva, in her radical deconstruction of the text and her questioning of accepted definitions of identity, opens the way for a future 'with heads and bodies finally liberated'.[6]

Feminist Literary Criticism Today

Feminist literary criticism now includes a lively combination of historical criticism, New Criticism, psychoanalysis, structuralism and deconstruction. The revisionary reading enhances our capacity to read the world, our literary texts, even one another. Literary criticism has been revitalised, in the way that many women writers felt born again with the Women's Liberation Movement. The women's movement spoke to lived as well as literary experience with the urgency of revelation. An intellectual revolution first exposed the

misogyny of critical practice and male stereotyping, then rediscovered a female tradition in literature, especially the novel. The
political movement developed at the same time as the literary; then
a female aesthetic emerged, based on women's culture and on styles
and forms related to female psychology. By the 1980s, a lesbian
aesthetic flourished, studying aspects of female sexuality, friendships and mother/daughter relationships – themes in many
women's novels, but viewed in new ways. Black feminist criticism is
establishing norms to examine the distinct cultural values of black
women writers, to prevent their being subsumed into 'universal'
literary studies, dominated by male and/or white writers.

The pluralism of feminist literary criticism is reflected in the
plurality of voices in women's novels today. Writers like Angela
Carter and Bessie Head consider the central conflict to be that
between men and women. Others, like Margaret Atwood and Alice
Walker, consider patriarchy a force equal to, and intertwined with
capitalism. With these writers, aspects of feminist criticism have
been absorbed into challenging novels.

Black women writers such as Alice Walker, Toni Morrison, Buchi
Emecheta write to shape their experience, and to reclaim both their
history and self-image, battered by their three enemies: racism,
classism, sexism. Though the division between male and female
roles emerges implicitly as they describe social situations and conditions, black women writers usually offer a *wider* critique of
patriarchy – in their struggle to find themselves and validate their
language. Most do not wish to be called feminist, a label which
might betray black men in a racist society, yet in their stories, a
critique of patriarchy emerges which represents female resistance to
male power. Many black women writers reclaim their mothers'
spoken discourse, giving value to both female and black oral
traditions.

The Diversity of Women's Writing

The French thinkers maintain that a woman writes 'with her body',
that is with rhythms reflecting unconscious and bodily drives;
whereas many British feminists claim that if anatomy is not destiny,
still less can it be language. They maintain that women have a
double vision, educated in the dominant (male) discourse, but able
to use subordinate discourse, which is now being revalued and
freed from taboos. The diversity of feminist literary criticism is even

more apparent in women's fictions, from those who refuse the label 'feminist', to those who use it to proclaim their intentions.

What do Angelou, Carter, Emecheta, Feinstein, Morrison, Rhys and Walker have in common? All share themes defined by Annette Kolodny as 'feminine', but apart from that they are vastly different.[7] They cannot be easily categorised, because they embrace a wide spectrum of fabulation and discourses, and slip in and out of feminist perspectives. These novelists represent a wide diversity of voices, many of whom are writing adventurous English, exploring their experiences in old and new forms. We see the continuing strengths of the women's novel since the eighteenth century, alongside experimentation. I believe we are moving towards a new history, a new literary criticism combining the experiences of men *and* women. In language we continually make new metaphors, create alternate meanings. The women novelists I have chosen represent a rich diversity of new metaphors and challenging meanings.

Notes

1   Arnold's 'typically English empiricist organicism' as Terry Eagleton describes it, reflects a tradition already developed by Coleridge. He drew heavily on both the radical empiricism of Hume and the transcendental subjective idealism of Kant. For an excellent survey of the significance of Kant's aesthetic judgements and their continuing sway (especially on the 'bourgeois' attitudes of Roger Scruton) see Christopher Norris, *Contest of Faculties* (1982), especially Chapter 5.

2   Apologies for assuming a binary opposition: Leavis=humanist, Saussure=anti-humanist. The arguments are tremendously complex; in fact, Derrida in *Of Grammatology* argues there is still a retention of 'logocentrism' in the privileged status which Saussure accords to speech (*parole*) where writing is designated to a suspect, supplementary status. Of course deconstruction as propounded by Derrida developed from Saussurian linguistics (and structuralism). But an implicit theme in many of Derrida's 'textual strategies' is the impossibility of drawing a clear demarcation between binary opposites. So Saussure's hierarchical levels, opposites, are not abandoned by deconstruction, but re-inscribed. Such arguments constitute part of the never-ending 'problematic' of the deconstruction project. I'd argue that Saussure, in his retention of a privileged status for *parole* as corresponding to truth and meaning in a seemingly unmediated manner, is not so opposed to a writer like Leavis as frequently assumed.

3   See Michael Ryan, *Marxism and Deconstruction*, Johns Hopkins Press, 1984.

4   See *New French Feminisms*, eds Marks and de Courtivron, Harvester Press, 1981.

5   Kristeva, 'Oscillation du "pouvoir" au "refus" ', *Tel Quel* 68, pp 98–102. Reprinted in *New French Feminisms*. To illustrate the imaginative use that can be made of these categories, I suggest one way of adapting them to Iris Murdoch: Kristeva claimed in *About Chinese Women* (1977, originally *Des Chinoises*, 1974) that a girl 'either identifies with her mother or raises herself to the symbolic stature of her father'. Murdoch could be said to have entered the symbolic order, accepting the Law of the Father which dominates much of our culture. This can produce contradictions in her work, between sexual fluidity and male psyches of narrators, between love of fantasy and respect for 'realism'.

6   Kristeva, 'Feminine Writing', in *New French Feminisms*, p 234.

7   See Annette Kolodny, 'A Map for Rereading', *New Literary History* 11: 3, pp 451–67. Kolodny suggests three shared attributes of those writings that can be defined as 'feminine': a reflexive perception, when the character is represented in activities not planned or situations not fully comprehended; inversion, when stereotyped literary images are turned round comically, reveal hidden identity, or connote their opposites; and fear of being trapped in inauthentic roles or fixed in false images which 'is the most compelling fear in women's fiction today'. I also recommend Kolodny's *The Lay of the Land: Metaphor as Experience in American Life and Letters*, University of North Carolina Press, 1975.

2
Angela Carter: Fantasist and Feminist

Angela Carter writes feminist fictions which are exhilaratingly useful reappraisals of women. In a didactic and playful manner, she uses fiction to explore attitudes to society and femininity. Her writing may baffle, even seem to assault the reader's sensibilities and beliefs, but her aims are constructive. None of her novels are 'realist', no character is believable, very few offer role-models. She creates *lies* – in order to bombard us with truths.

As Marxist and French feminist critics recommend, Carter breaks down academic (male) divisions between 'good' and 'bad' literature; popular forms of literature such as science fiction and detective stories are treated seriously. Both Carter and Doris Lessing use science fiction, though in differing ways, to explore possible futures. Carter examines the possibility of a female community, headed by a mythical Mother in *The Passion of New Eve*, or run by lesbian prisoners in *Nights at the Circus*.

She explores the destructiveness of fantasising. In this, her writing is similar to Iris Murdoch's, but differs in depicting the self-absorption of desire rather than its leading to love. Fantasies interfere with the ability to relate to the 'otherness' of others. As the heroine of *Heroes and Villains* remarks, 'I shall never know how he *really* looks ...'.

In her early novels she delights in taking a conventional adolescent heroine and 'putting her through the mangle'* in order to examine the position of the virtuous woman. Carter believes that 'hoping good behaviour will bring its own reward is not moral but sentimental, and inadequate in resisting oppression.'* When Carter represents a powerful woman, such as de Sade's Juliette, she shows her avoiding slavery by embracing tyranny. 'A free woman in an unfree society is a monster', she contends in *The Sadeian Woman* (1979). These polemical insights inform her work's ability to infuriate or stimulate.

* denotes author's conversation with Angela Carter, 3 August 1985.

Carter has supplemented her experience of male, academic discourse with enthusiastic, unconventional reading in other genres. By manipulating these genres, she exalts women's traditions, by looking at their subcultures, in dialogue and in imagery, and at the marginal, at the circus, at freaks, at unacknowledged areas.

She often re-tells old stories, filling in 'the bits that got left out', and pirates past literature to embroider her fictional points. Fairy tales, nursery rhymes, and children's stories provide an opportunity to re-think assumptions by examining 'old lies and seeing how they are made into new lies'. The folk-tale is preferred to classical myth, the lumber-room of the imagination to the unconscious. In *The Company of Wolves*, the popular story of Red Riding Hood is turned on its head: the wolves symbolise the girl's awakening sexuality, while the male ego is mocked.

Since the 1970s, she has foregrounded women's experiences, through female languages and the intuitive aspects of female intelligence. In doing so, she demonstrates that females have the power to refuse to subscribe to male meanings. In *Black Venus* (1985) Carter rescues Jeanne Duval from Baudelaire's myths about her. But she does not simply de-mythologise Duval, she *re*-mythologises her, as a home-loving black prostitute instead of an extraordinary male ideal. Carter re-mythologises with an exuberant humour which appeals as much to men as to women. Society no longer excludes women from any comic discourse – bawdy jokes, slapstick and sexual innuendo not excepted. Writers like Angela Carter have done what feminist linguist Deborah Cameron recommends: change outward practice so that a choice of metaphor subverts a social institution.

Early Life and Work

In her autobiographical essay in *Nothing Sacred* (Virago, 1982), Carter characterises her upbringing as 'governed by the women in the family'. Born in 1940, she left school out of boredom, suffered a brief period of anorexia, married and went to Bristol University at the age of 22. She began her writing career as a journalist on the *Croydon Advertiser*. In the late 1960s, she was radicalised through her emotional and sexual experiences, and two of her works are consciously informed by feminism: the novel *The Passion of New Eve* (1977) and *The Sadeian Woman and the Ideology of Pornography: An Exercise in Cultural History* (1979). Together with these works, she has written eight other novels displaying unusual diversity of imagination, three collections of bizarre short stories, and various idiosyncratic articles. This chapter analyses Carter's innovative features, followed by a chronological account of her fiction.

In both fiction and non-fiction she examines the cultural construction of femininity with imaginative contentiousness, and questions our socially determined norms. Carter states her aims incisively:

> It is enormously important for women to write fiction as women, it is part of the slow process of decolonialising our language. We must work to develop a neutral language, without pain, shame or embarrassment. Language is power, life and the instrument of culture, the instrument of domination and liberation.*

She feels an affinity with those Third World writers who are aiming to change perceptions through fiction, and particularly admires the South African writer Bessie Head, who uses forms utterly alien to her own historical culture to produce complex illustrations of sexual and political struggle:

> In my work I keep saying that women are people too ... values are determined by a specific sex and class and I think it's unjust. And in order to think about these things you've got to have the language to do it.[1]

For Angela Carter, growing into feminism was part of her maturing as a writer: 'The Women's Movement made me what I am. Though I write for anyone who will read me, in a sense I'm writing for my sisters.'*

While novelists like Margaret Drabble were concentrating on women's domestic situations, Carter was examining the potential of the feminist novel by combining the phantasmagoric with the realistic. Having studied the French surrealists Alfred Jarry and André Breton, she has used images from sources as disparate as medieval allegory and the films of Fellini to reflect and to precipitate changes in the way people, and especially women, feel about themselves.

By the late 1970s, her anxious experiments of the 1960s had given way to more assured and exuberant explorations. *The Passion of New Eve* (1977) brilliantly deconstructs male attitudes to femininity, and *Nights at the Circus* (1984) is a flamboyant, multi-faceted depiction of a 'new woman', a study of women's experience through the life of an 'artiste' and courtesan.

Carter is fascinated by the ways in which we construct ideas of ourselves under the pressures of socialisation: the conscious and unconscious forces which constrain and channel our perceptions of reality and the fractured subjectivity with which we are left. To Carter, 'fiction is fiction' and should interpret everyday reality through a system of imagery derived from subterranean areas behind everyday experience. To this end she favours the use of the fantastical: folklore, fairytale, gothic, fabulous medieval romance. Their symbolic narrative appeals at the conscious and subconscious levels. At the same time, her intention is not only to entertain but also to instruct, and she uses various literary devices to that purpose, for example, the picaresque, where 'people have adventures in order to find themselves in places where they can discuss philosophical concepts'.*

Her narrative tends to allow bizarre extravagances of plot. While this may alienate the more traditionally-minded reader, her work appeals to science fiction devotees who are accustomed to the extravagant as a means to study possible futures or to illuminate the complexities of the present. Many academic critics still fail to take science fiction seriously enough. Yet, as a genre, it allows writers the structural freedom to explore new concepts. Carter's best novels add elements of science fiction to a range of sources from the phantasmagoric to the naturalistic, to project both the inner life of her characters, and a critique of the social world.

The phantasmagoric and the naturalistic are linked in her approach to landscape: the parks in *The Magic Toyshop* and *Love* are places with which she is familiar, and which she transforms into moonlit, surreal backgrounds, invoking crazy reactions in her characters. Seedy streets express organic social disintegration: 'crumbling in decay, overladen with the desolate burden of humanity' (*The Magic Toyshop*, p 98). The English countryside exudes melancholy: 'A cold day of late October, when the withered blackberries dangled like their own dour spooks on the discoloured brambles' (*The Bloody Chamber*, p 84). The American desert is wild in itself and a projection of the protagonist's emotions: 'An insane landscape of pale rock, honeycombed peak upon peak in unstable, erratic structures, calcified assemblages of whiteness and silence where jostling pebbles marked the paths of rivers dried up before time began' (*The Passion of New Eve*, p 45). 'I have this idea', Carter says, 'that if you describe something absolutely precisely, someone else can see it in the same way.'*

Throughout her work, Carter uses literary and cinematic allusions, to widen themes and to demonstrate the extent to which our ideas are shaped by our culture. 'Life imitating rotten art again', remarks one of her characters. Stereotypes, such as the baby doll or the 'macho' in black leather, are used in an ironic manner, to illustrate the pressures of subconscious socialisation. The ironic approach is inherently dangerous: 'when using irony', she concedes, 'one is on a knife edge between parody and seriousness.'* In *The Passion of New Eve* she uses pastiches of film sequences to underline the maiming of female personality by idealisation of Hollywood icons.

She shocks us by mocking role-identification and the 'realism' of male viewpoints. The reality that circumscribes women is subversively surveyed through the symbols of exploitation and sexual gratification. Carter considers that

> a critique of these symbols is a critique of our lives. Gender is a state of mind as much as anything else. We are echo chambers. I'm not worried about alienating readers by all my allusions, as science fiction addicts are quite prepared to look up things they don't know. But of course I was educated at a time when one could take a shared culture for granted.*

Certain objects are given symbolic value and recur throughout her work: mirrors, colours, the moon, cosmetics, fire (or its absence), dolls, knives, and especially garments. Clothes represent an expression of cultural pressure. In *The Passion of New Eve* all the women in Zero's harem are dressed alike; Jewel, the assertive tribal male of *Heroes and Villains*, wears jewels, feathers and warpaint. Young heroines wear richly detailed wedding dresses, so ancient that they crumble 'like Miss Haversham's. I always use it ironically when something terrible is about to happen.'[2]

Mirrors also appear frequently, objectifying us being looked at by ourselves. Asked if she were influenced here by Borges, Carter replied, 'Slightly, but more by Cocteau in his films'.* Mirrors, however, in Cocteau's work are pathways to the underworld and to immortality, while Carter's mirrors are self-reflecting tyrannical prisons. Mirrors are surreal, reflecting a face one may no longer wish to see. Melanie, at the beginning of *The Magic Toyshop*, feels impelled to shatter her mirror. Carter perceives the mirror as inimical because it lures a woman into complicity with her fate by enabling her to see herself as others do – and spend energy trying to change.

Carter admires Sophia (wisdom) in *The Passion of New Eve* because she 'looked like a woman who has never seen a mirror in all her life; not once exposed herself to those looking-glasses that betray women into nakedness' (p 54). Her opposite is Leilah who first appears as a sex object, dressed meat, having transformed herself with make-up, furs and high heels. Mirrors take this night-club dancer into 'the self-created, self-perpetuating solipsistic world of the woman watching herself being watched' (p 30). Yet, away from mirrors, Leilah blossoms into a full personality, freed from sexual stereotyping.

Her love of fantasy might prevent readers from perceiving social attitudes until they realise that the images can be taken literally: in *Nights at the Circus* (1984) the heroine has wings; she is a metaphor come to life so that Carter can expatiate on what would happen to a woman who is both winged spirit and Winged Victory.

Fiction is not true, therefore anything can happen, once you establish the rules of what you're inventing. There are certain things I can only say in metaphorical language which involves the unreal, such as the unreality of fairy-tale. I let ideas spark off one another.[3]

The ideas are sparked off with a disconcerting mingling of horror, comedy, and eroticism.

Carter's earlier novels studied corrupting passivity, the decay of experience into dream and fantasy, and the charisma exerted by a powerful male. Her pubescent heroines experienced a perverse need to cling to a being who both attracts and repels, as is often found in gothic novels. *The Magic Toyshop* (1967) is an adolescent girl's discovery of her sexuality – and urban sordidness – through a skilfully crafted gothic fairy-tale. Carter became more boldly imaginative in *Heroes and Villains* (1969) dealing with the survival of impoverished groups after a nuclear holocaust. *Love* (1971), realistically anchored in a seedy bohemian milieu, examines the relationship between love and insanity: 'The derangement of views of reality is a recurring theme of mine.'[*]

Science fiction fans praised *The Infernal Desire Machines of Doctor Hoffman* (1972), a speculation on the destruction of rationality. In this novel, Carter presents a hero who is unable to internalise a role thrust upon him from without.

The Magic Toyshop

The Magic Toyshop appeared in 1967, the year Gabriel García Marquez's novel *One Hundred Years of Solitude* was published. Carter considers that the success of Marquez prepared the public to accept her writing. Both Marquez and Carter have been called 'magic realists'. They attribute to places and people experiences both local and more broadly characteristic. They recreate history imaginatively: Carter investigates the treatment of women, Marquez the recurrent civil wars and depredations of Latin America. They both proclaim their novels as literary objects in a larger situation, exorcising the past, occasionally pointing to a different future.

Though not as sweeping in imaginative scope as Marquez's novels, *The Magic Toyshop* moves skilfully between fantasy and reality: 'Mrs Rundle would sit ... dreamily inventing the habits and behaviour of the husband she had never enjoyed until his very face formed wispily in the steam from her bed-time cup of tea.' (p 3) This prepares us for a world where people live their fantasies, sometimes gently, sometimes grotesquely, like Uncle Philip with his life-sized dolls.

Melanie, one of Carter's pubescent heroines, is a beautiful girl of fifteen who is undergoing the process of adopting societal images to form her adult self: 'Pre-Raphaelite, she combed out her long black hair ... a la Toulouse-Lautrec, she dragged her hair sluttishly along her face.' (p 1) 'She gift-wrapped herself for a phantom bridegroom ... she could almost feel his breath on her cheek ... Venice. Or Miami Beach.' (p 2)

Her adolescent self-deceptions are interrupted when her parents are killed in a plane crash. She and her orphaned brothers find themselves destitute, and the only relative to offer them a roof is the ogre-like Uncle Philip. Echoes of fairytale underpin the plot: Melanie must undergo a series of painful experiences before she is finally rescued. 'This investigation of the social fictions that regulate our lives – what Blake called "mind forg'd manacles" – is what I've concerned myself with consciously.'[4]

In the new household, Melanie is dragged from her fictions to the harsh reality of the unwashed Irish step-brother Finn. Without mirrors, she loses her self-identity; she witnesses cruelty, malevolence, incestuous intrigue, loneliness. The new Irish relatives are recognisable only as types, not as individuals. They play the fiddle and flute; they have wild red hair and recall pagan celtic deities. They also suffer from morning to night, exploited by Uncle Philip. 'In order to question the nature of reality one must move from a strongly-grounded base in what constitutes material reality.'[5] The seedy house and the huge, menacing Uncle Philip comprise the material reality, from which it is possible to study the power and repulsion exercised by a tyrannical human being.

Manipulation is pervasive both in society and in literature. Melanie, initially, is the young woman who accepts the limited stereotypical images offered by advertising and by culture. Uncle Philip is the arbiter of this stereotyping: his 'Puppet Microcosm' indicates the macabre way he wishes to manipulate the world.

The Female Gothic

Both Uncle Philip and Melanie are characters whose origins lie in the gothic novel. In the gothic novel, a tyrannical male, charismatic and/or demonic, looms over the central figure, a young woman, who is both persecuted victim and courageous heroine. Many outstanding gothic novels were written by women and gave both women characters and readers an adventurous release from their powerless social situation and a chance to explore their hidden potential.

In spite of the widespread appeal of melodrama and horror, this women's genre was derided and half-submerged for decades. This dismissal of the genre is symptomatic of the undervaluing of women's writing that has only been redressed recently by feminist critics. The gothic novel is seen now as a versatile instrument for probing aspects of male malevolence and female sexuality. Ellen Moers in *Literary Women* (1977) demonstrates the many themes included in this vital female tradition.[6]

The first gothic novel was *The Castle of Otranto* (1764) written by Horace Walpole, but the popularity of the genre was achieved by Mrs Ann Radcliffe with *The Mysteries of Udolpho: A Romance* (1794). In this novel we have the elements now associated with the term 'gothic': a gloomy castle or country house with underground passages and half-hidden attics; a lonely heroine, often persecuted; a heartless, domineering aristocratic villain; the arousing of fear, by natural and supernatural events.

Fantasy predominates over everyday reality, as in Carter's work. The opening landscape of *The Mysteries of Udolpho* reveals symbolic effects both delight in: 'Summits, veiled in clouds, or exhibiting awful forms, gleamed through the blue tinge of air and sometimes frowned with forests of gloomy pine' (p 1). Mrs Radcliffe uses the vocabulary of the picturesque to heighten the lyrical or terrifying moments. She inaugurated elements women employed in many subsequent novels, such as scenery and sentiment, scarcely mentioned by Defoe or Richardson.

She combined a sense of mystery with a prevailing love of the grand and wonderful, yet underpinned her fantasies with sensible moral judgements. This moral sense, based on the values of eighteenth-century rationalism, speeded her wide acceptance. Her heroines travel abroad, visiting castles and mansions, gaining a freedom of movement seldom granted to women by society. In the areas of this inner and outer space, they are confronted with rational and irrational fears. Only by conquering the irrational and exposing illusions can they tackle real dangers. At a time when young women seldom travelled, the gothic novel sent them on imaginary journeys, with implicit criticism of the men who attempt to ensnare them. Many of these elements appear in Carter's exultantly gothic *Nights at the Circus*.

The gothic novel gained in strength with the onset of the Romantic movement, since it extolled the imagination. It unleashed women's imaginative powers, enabling them to show women acting boldly and with their wits about them. In gloomy confines, female repression is highlighted dramatically, with implicit praise for the qualities of resourcefulness displayed.

The female artist must destroy part of herself, 'the angel in the house', in order to create. The stress caused is turned into frightening myth by Mary Shelley in *Frankenstein* (1818). Her novel, bordering on science fiction, transforms her own maternal fears over childbirth, together with the gothic ingredients of infanticide and incest, into a nightmare. She is a 'terrorist of the imagination', Carter's term for those who, like de Sade, create myths out of unpleasant sexual fantasies in order to make society face them. The myth of Frankenstein is particularly suitable for a feminist writer: the creation takes on a larger life, attacking society.

The gothic plot was mocked by Jane Austen in *Northanger Abbey* (1818) but taken up eagerly by the Brontës in their childhood stories of Angria and Gondal. Though she disciplined her later writing, Charlotte could not expunge completely the gothic influence. Indeed, the incarceration of mad Bertha Mason in the attic in *Jane Eyre* goes far beyond melodrama. She becomes a frightening image of society's punishment of what were considered excessive female sexual instincts. *Wuthering Heights* (1847) extends the imaginative significance of the gothic when it accepts the cruel as normal. Wracked with the melodramatic passions of the gothic, it is a masterpiece of romantic fiction, spiritual profundity and shrewd realism.

Carter is proud of working in this tradition of gothic fiction. 'At first, the label "gothic" helped to give me intellectual respectability, then it marginalised me and now it has become respectable again.'* The form is useful since characterisation and style invite exaggeration, thus operating against 'the perennial human desire to believe the word and world as fact'.* The increasingly bizarre extravagance of her plots might suggest the label 'camp-gothic'. With an almost Brechtian use of alienation, she indulges in pastiche, with enthusiastic, sometimes vulgar agility. This cerebral approach is essential for a writer concerned with self-creation under the menace of destruction, as in *The Magic Toyshop*.

Carter's Middle Period

In *Heroes and Villains*, a fable about a post-nuclear future, Carter extends the elements of gothic and magic realism. A few favoured professors live in concrete blocks, protected by barbed wire, perpetuating a culture only they can understand. Out in the open live marauding tribes, using a language reduced to the minimum needed for survival. Carter juxtaposes the apocalyptic with the everyday to envisage how we might fit into such a future.

She conveys this vision of a devastated future:

> Long ago the sea wrenched apart the massive blocks of an esplanade ... then swirled through abandoned thoroughfares nibbling, gobbling, gulping and digesting stone, brick and stucco. Now incurious fish swam in bedrooms where submerged mirrors reflected faces no more, only the mazy dance of wrack and wreckage. (p 138)

She speculates, with sensitivity to contemporary theory, on what would happen to our vision if our language were destroyed: 'Losing their names, these things underwent a process of uncreation and reverted to chaos, existing only to themselves in an unstructured world.' (p 137)

Carter switches from time to timelessness, imparting a sense of wonder, humour, and threatening horror. Her heroine, Marianne, finds ordered life so boring that she joins the Barbarians. She is made the wife of the leader, Jewel, who maintains his authority partly by his impressive decoration of jewels, feathers, metal and paint. She cannot internalise the Barbarians' codes and uses her intelligence to survive. 'When she perceived she and her Jewel were in some way related to one another she was filled with pain for her idea of her own autonomy. However, might not such a conviction serve her as well as proven certainty?' (p 132) She adapts unwillingly to the roles thrust upon her: first Evil, then totem, finally wife and mother. Finally she exploits her cunning to become leader: 'I'll be the tiger lady and rule them with a rod of iron.' (p 150) Whether she achieves this is left unresolved. The final word is 'silence'.

Heroes and Villains displays some of the qualities of Doris Lessing's *Memoirs of a Survivor* (1974). Both shift from realism to magic to study a time when barbarism becomes normality, analysing the fight for sustenance and the ultimate descent into murder. Both create metaphors for a society where sexuality is dominated by tribal males but where the women survive by their wits and their power of adaptability.

In a departure from both magic realism and the gothic, Carter wrote the bleak novel *Love* in 1971. The novel is a 'tragedy of contemporary manners ... a total analysis of a complex emotional situation, leaving nothing out and being as honest as possible'. Through the character of Annabel, Carter explores the private world of the insane. 'I had just read Laing and Foucault who influenced me to make the nature of reality a central issue.' As they suffer and undermine those who love them but cannot reach them, the mentally ill characters feel doomed by acute self-awareness. Carter bases the novel in Bristol while taking us into the minds of people shut up in the intensity of their emotions:

> One day Annabel saw the sun and moon in the sky at the same time. The sight filled her with a terror that entirely consumed her and did not leave her until the night closed in catastrophe for she had no instinct for self-preservation if she was confronted by ambiguities. (p 7)

The Infernal Desire Machines of Doctor Hoffman (1972) chronicles Desiderio's struggle not to be blasted 'to non-being by the ferocious artillery of non-reason'. Almost alone he fights the Determination Police who 'break all the lawless mirrors' and the spooks used by Doctor Hoffman as guerillas. Asked if the images of violence and desire reveal the workings of our unconscious, the Id, Carter replied, 'Partly, but they are also aspects of the popular material I use: B movies, newspapers, ballads. The end is an elaborate parody of James Bond films.'*

After bizarre adventures Hoffman's secret is discovered, in his laboratory where couples endlessly copulate in wire cages. This macabre fable is a grotesquely humorous parody of the dehumanisation of intimate relationships whenever they are exploited for material motives. *The Infernal Desire Machines of Doctor Hoffman* is also an example of how Carter uses literary styles to examine contemporary cultural theories. In this case, Carter is also poking fun at Wilhelm Reich's theories of sexual therapy.

A Feminist Novel

With inventive wit and an extravagant plot, Carter wrote *The Passion of New Eve* (1977), which plays a serious surrealist game in order to explore the tyranny of cultural myths. 'We must not blame our poor symbols if they take forms that seem trivial or absurd, for the symbols themselves have no control over their fleshly manifestations; the nature of our life has determined their forms.' (p 6)

Carter emphasises here, as in *The Sadeian Woman* (1979), that cultural interpretations of sexuality can and do change. She displays a deftness with stereotypes enhanced by her ability to imbue them with individualised reactions. The protagonist is at first a man, later transformed into a woman, obsessed with the Hollywood star Tristessa. Tristessa, like Garbo, has willingly subsumed her personality into myth. 'It's about Hollywood and the way it's affected so many aspects of our lives, especially sexuality.'*

The Passion of New Eve was written after Carter visited the United States. She combines her reactions to American society with speculation about a future where the women's movement and the black power movement are taken much further than the present, into a visionary future where women and blacks refuse to be governed. She had 'previously wanted to be more political, but only with this novel found a suitable form'.*

The novel opens with a portrayal of the parasitic relationship 'the man' inflicts upon Leilah, a black whore, in New York City. ('The man' is unnamed in the novel, but is later re-made as the new Eve.) At first he can only see Leilah as a projection of his libidinous fantasy. She is the 'profane essence of the death of cities' (p 18), longing for sensuality: not for its own sake but to be exorcised by it. As Leilah dresses for her dance routine in night-clubs she sees herself in mirrors, reflecting male desiderata of false eyelashes, purple tits and lips: 'Her beauty was an accession, arrived at by conscious effort.' (p 28) Carter again stresses self-construction and the damage it inflicts: 'She brought into being a Leilah who lived only in the not-world of the mirror.' (p 28) The man is unable to appreciate Leilah as a person: his love-making deliberately parodies pornography. In *The Sadeian Woman*, Carter comments, 'Pornography has an inbuilt reactionary mechanism ... it reinforces false universals of sexual archetypes.' (p 16)

When Leilah becomes pregnant and wants to have the baby, the man feels betrayed and angry. He flees to the desert, where he is captured and led to Beulah, an underground women's commune. Its name is taken from William Blake's Beulah 'where contrarieties exist together. Since its blueprint is a state of mind, it has the unimpeachable quality of realism. But it is a triumph of science and hardly anything about is natural.' (p 49) Beulah's head is Mother, a black fertility goddess who 'has made symbolism a concrete fact, a self-constructed theology' (p 58).

The chambers of Beulah are plastic spheres, like science-fiction chapels. Here the protagonist undergoes surgery and is made into a female. Now the new Eve must learn to become a woman, in much the same spirit as Simone de Beauvoir's observation of 1949, that women are made, not born. The new Eve views slides of suckling mammals and videos of Madonnas, and then she is forced to marry Tristessa – who is revealed to be a man.

The disclosure of Tristessa's true gender is evidence that only a man can successfully incarnate the image he would like a woman to become. When she worked in Japan, Carter saw Kabuki theatre, where men impersonate women with such skill that they can appear too perfect, proof of the feminist thesis of the mutability of sexual character and gender identity. The love-making between Tristessa and Eve represents an ideal where the male and female characteristics in each person are recognised. 'We had made the great Platonic hermaphrodite together ... we brought into being the being who stops time in the self-created eternity of lovers.' (p 148) Carter makes an interesting observation on her method: 'Eve and Tristessa must have an ecstatic coupling here, because it's fiction. They deserve a *Liebestod* before Tristessa is murdered.'*

Eve emerges from the desert to find women and blacks winning their revolutionary war against white men. She discovers Leilah to be the leader: a wise, intelligent person now that she is no longer a male-oriented sex object. 'History overtook myth.' (p 172) The cities of California are burning, purged like all man-made gods. This visionary message merges with symbolic story-telling: Eve undergoes an ordeal to prepare for the future. She struggles through caves to reach the seashore and fresh horizons. In the caves Eve goes back through eons of evolutionary time to realise that the word 'progression' was just as meaningless as the word 'duration' (p 183). By the ocean, 'mother of mysteries', she finds Mother, now a gentle old lady, 'flotsam of time', singing to herself. 'Mother is a figure of speech and has retired to a cave beyond consciousness.' (p 184) With this image Carter demonstrates one of the ideas of *The Sadeian Woman*: 'Myth deals in false universals, to dull the pain of the particular … It is consolatory nonsense.' (p 5)

The novel ends with visions of a new world where a lonely Eve learns to live on, unaided by myth or commune. Carter has welded a range of concepts into an extravagant plot, to construct a subversive feminist fable.

Short Stories

Carter has published several volumes of short stories, or tales, as she prefers to call them. 'The tale does not log everyday experience as the short story does: it interprets through a system of imagery derived from subterranean areas, and therefore cannot betray its readers into false knowledge.' (*Fireworks* (1974), p 121) In one tale, she examines socialisation through a puppet who is so much more vital than her weak, ageing manipulator that she vampirises him. The horror fantasy is treated ironically as the puppet enjoys no real autonomy and ends her life in the local brothel. The tales in *The Bloody Chamber* (1979) are modern re-workings of fairy stories and folk tales, exploring different kinds of consciousness and female sexuality through archetypal characters and situations.

The first and longest tale in *The Bloody Chamber* is based on the tale of Bluebeard. The modern Bluebeard is a rich, handsome, middle-aged banker, who can afford to marry impoverished girls and dispose of them when they show signs of disobedience. The style deliberately mocks romance: 'I lay awake in the *wagon-lit* in a tender, delicious ecstasy of excitement, my burning cheek pressed against the impeccable linen of my pillow.' (p 7) Carter creates a distance between the reader and the text to make us accept the amusing, yet horrifying, recreation of sado-masochistic dreams.

Each tale is resonant of the folk-mode from which it is derived. *Puss-in-Boots* uses the first person in an intimate yet farcical tone that recreates the medieval tale: 'For what lady in the world could say "no" to the passionate yet discreet advances of a fine marmalade cat?' (p 68) *The Werewolf* is a re-working of Little Red Riding Hood and examines cruelty and cunning: 'It is a northern country; they have cold weather, they have cold hearts; when they discover a witch ... they stone her to death.' (p 108) Fairy story uses symbolic actions to bypass the censorship of the conscious mind. It is a useful tool to articulate problems without the prescriptive character of myth, which Carter finds limiting in comparison. Contradictory reactions to sexuality can be presented more concisely in tales than in the elaborate discourse of works of criticism such as *The Sadeian Woman*. Thus the red rose in *The Lady of the House of Love* symbolises sexual love and malignity. Its beauty is obscene, fertilised by the remains of vampirised victims.

In 1984, the tale *The Company of Wolves* was made into an acclaimed feature film. Four magical stories take place in a wild wood where subconscious terrors are exposed and explored. The pubescent heroine has archetypal dreams about folk-tale wolves: 'These wolves represent aspects of her own developing adolescent libido.'* The grandmother, partly based on Carter's own story-telling grandmother, utters proverbial wisdom. Eventually we reach the adult conclusion that a wolf is no more frightening than a 'man with red eyes in whose unkempt mane the lice moved' (p 118). The film fuses the elements of toytown and sinister horror, images we have all seen on television since childhood, and which readily produce a response in us. Carter's stylish literary metaphors are transformed into powerful visual and emotional images.

The New Woman

In *Nights at the Circus* (1984), Carter takes the image of the angel and examines what would happen if a woman actually did possess wings. Fevvers is a fantastic heroine, born with wings; she is a six foot tall music hall artiste who was hatched from an egg and brought up in a brothel. 'I wanted her to be wonderful and not very nice, like Mae West, one of my heroines. The sort of person who usually comes to a bad end.'* This is an allegory of woman as wonder and worker of wonders, a fabulous winged creation, impli-citly critical of the fantasies of the Id.*

Set in the year 1899, the novel takes place in a circus, and examines society from the viewpoint of outsiders: women and freaks.

I chose 1899 because it's almost 100 years since then to the end of *this* century *and* because she's [Fevvers] a *new* woman. Though she seems abnormal to others, she's normal to herself. She is a symbolic woman, not just an exhibition in a museum of curiosities.[7]

Fevvers opens the story by giving an account of her fantastic life to a young American journalist, who combines 'professional necessity to see all and believe nothing with characteristically American generosity towards the brazen lie'. (p 10) His habitual disengagement is shattered by the erotic charms of Fevvers, who is literally larger than life with an enormous comforting bosom. She has used her freakish charms to break out of brutal brothels, and now does so to work out her own female salvation. Carter takes the angle of examining the world as seen by freaks: 'but these women freaks in brothels are more normal than the men who visit them, who are in trouble with their souls.'*

The narrative drive is greater here than in previous novels. The plot moves from London music halls to St. Petersburg to a surreal Siberia, inhabited by Siberian tribesmen for whom, like Carter herself, there is no difference between fact or fiction.

She fuses her love of fantasy with subtle, half-concealed political comment, producing the character of Lizzie, Fevvers' Marxist foster mother. Lizzie is an unbusiness-like prostitute who lectures her clients on the white slave trade, the rights and wrongs of women, and universal suffrage. She is the 'portable rationalist. One needs people one can consult. Especially as a girl – I was always being given the wrong advice.'*

But Fevvers refuses to believe Lizzie, the sensible Marxist reminding her about class and the dangers of false consciousness. The tale ends with Fevvers making love to Walser, the journalist, she on top because of her wings. We are left not knowing if she is laughing loudly from real joy or because she still feels she must pretend to be the archetypal woman. The story suggests the possibility of taking off, interwoven with the limitations women still feel in the twentieth century. In the end, Fevvers has become a plain sparrow, but is this diminishing – or more real than her painted nineteenth-century self? The images examine both female potential, through Fevvers' exploits, and male stereotyping of women, from Sleeping Beauty to the willing masochist. Elements of gothic melodrama combine with the picaresque.

The picaresque has enabled the writer, from Cervantes onwards, to invent ludicrous adventures to entertain, while moralising on the state of the world or the limitations of the human mind. Carter considers the allegory political because the circus is an arena for emblematic beings to perform their acts. These allegorical beings must entertain their audiences and make us laugh – as the novelist does, near the end of the novel, when we come to the picaresque element: 'all those who are alive move into the wilderness, victims of a train crash, so that they can have long discussions about life.'*

Carter believes that we use the 'imagination' to hide from the dark side of ourselves. Thus she plunders art and writing in order to highlight the grotesque in an attempt to reject the 'prettification' of the 'imagination'. (The title of her selection of journalism *Nothing Sacred* accurately describes her piratical approach.) She appropriates past fictions, in part to send up false legends. In *Nights at the Circus* she has rejected much erotic heritage, while creating a New Woman of her own. She makes explicit the harsh or carnal subtext of what she borrows, yet is alive to the decorative element in myth-making. Much of Carter's force derives from exposing these conflicts in pirated texts.

Her explicit aim is for women to 'have wings, tear off their mind-forg'd manacles, open their cages and close brothels'.* Fevvers represents the lives of all women who have been marginalised, as courtesans, as performers. Carter validates the almost forgotten achievements of women performers, on stage, on tour, on show. She considers that women performers were allowed to work in amazingly arduous conditions. For example, at a time when society protected middle class women, Clara Schumann was still playing in piano concerts when she was eight months pregnant! Though marginalised, some women acquired power, some money, while others created women's communities which gave them warmth and independence, 'a sub-text of fertility beneath the glittering sterility of the pleasure of the flesh' (p 262).

Black Venus

Black Venus, published in 1985, breaks new ground and was praised by many critics. Carter combines the versatility of her journalism with imaginings about unusual characters, both real and fictional, to produce what are really poetic meditations, though termed short stories. When she first read Jorge Luis Borges' works, she found them liberating and exciting. His unusual, half-philosophical short stories are linked with the speculative and didactic medieval material she admired and utilised. In *Black Venus*, she has also included pastiches of different styles from the abstruse to the vulgar, creating a new genre and furthermore a brand new intertextuality in these witty disquisitions.

Lisa St Aubin de Terán praises Carter as a

poet of the short story. The eight pieces in *Black Venus* focus on the seven deadly sins. We accept a split-level technique, a vein of historicising enquiry, cheerfully vandalising criticism to erect a new kind of *nouveau roman*. One of the surprises is that the stories which appear entirely fictive are presented with the same attractively spurious verve of authority as the truer tales.[8]

In the title story, *Black Venus*, Carter conjures up the emotional life of a woman existing only on the margins of male literature – Jeanne Duval, Baudelaire's black Venus. Her representation is brilliant and empathetic: 'Jeanne was like a piano in a country where everyone has had their hands cut off.' (p 9) Carter gives Jeanne a mythical genealogy. Baudelaire sees her as exotic mistress, symbol of corrupting sensuality, 'black-thighed witch'. Carter represents her, by employing various differing registers, as double victim, robbed of her African heritage by French imperialism, and even more demeaning, robbed of her unpretentious humanity by the poet's fantasising of her. She imagines Jeanne speaking a patois which Baudelaire the poet does not share; his beautiful poems are in a language which alienates her from her own experience and leaves her dumb. 'The greatest poet of alienation stumbled upon the perfect stranger; theirs was a match made in heaven.' (p 18)

The Fall River Axe Murders is another meditation on a marginalised, 'mythologised' woman – Lizzie Borden, the nineteenth-century axe murderer. Carter read the transcript of Borden's trial and manages to evoke her thoughts during the exhausting dog days before the murders, while presenting a straightforward depiction of the claustrophobia of a southern Massachusetts mill town. Significantly, the actual murders are left out of this claustrophobic and compassionate study. She is skilful in conveying the *materiality* of imaginative life: the circumscribed life of women, the lust for money, the unpleasant decaying smells of the past. In this story, she is a committed materialist, yet paradoxically chooses 'magicking or making everything strange' in other stories.

In *Peter and the Wolf*, the girl suckled by wolves decides to stay with them rather than join the human race. In *Overture and Incidental Music to A Midsummer Night's dream*, Carter recreates the figure of Puck, meditating on the Changeling (who makes everything go wrong) and Victorian versions of fairies: 'The Victorians did not leave the woods in quite the state they might have wished to find them.' (p 69) She opens her story with crudely erotic glee – 'Call me the Golden Herm' – and continues with an ironic meditation on 'the whole of western European culture as if it were an oral tradition'.*

Carter conflates contradictions in her non-naturalistic writing because 'narrative is an argument stated in fictional terms'.* Her power stems from such fusing of opposites, an urge towards earthiness *and* a wish to take off, like Fevvers. She invites her readers to continue interpreting her characters 'as if they were real ... to take one step further into the fictionality of the narrative, instead of coming out of it and looking at it as though it were an artefact'.*

As a result, her artifice can appear too opulent and mannerist. She admits she is sometimes cursed by fluency, by enthusiasm for 'magicking'. But all her stories, including those for children, reveal skill in linking magic with polemic, visual imagery with comedy. These are tales for our time: the bizarre extravagances of plot are purposely artificial and cerebral to demonstrate our playing of parts, our process of unwitting self-creation.

Conclusion

Carter counters myth with myth. 'The reward for careful reading is a shock of recognition, the attribution of a significance which we can situate in contemporary life and contemporary reading.'[9] Her skill in creating characters has been termed 'Frankensteinish' since she makes them subsume roles, exchange roles, even sexes, with monstrous agility. 'Their rootlessness, the strangeness, vulgarity and arbitrariness of the ideas they use to interpret the times are harder, now, to classify as eccentricities.'[10]

Her theatricality heightens the parody of social attitudes and myths of femininity. The artificiality and cerebral quality of her writing is designed to alienate. Such 'alienation' is not a symptom of the inadequacy of her characterisation (as some critics maintain) but an essential tool to challenge cultural constructs.

At the same time, her texts can be interpreted with the same alacrity that dreams can be interpreted with. One can be both in and outside dream (and nightmare) in the way Carter shifts in and out of criticism of her text. She admits, 'My fiction is often a kind of literary criticism. I had spent time happily acquiescing in Borges' idea that books were about books.' But then she boldly broke out of that literary universe to exploit our whole European literary heritage as 'a kind of folklore'. Her literary extravagance is intent on giving 'materiality to imaginative life and imaginative experience which should be taken quite seriously'.[11] She exaggerates comic devices to represent the way characters and events can be made into symbols and ideas. Thus her discourse appears overwrought, even unnatural at times, in order to 'operate against the perennial desire to believe the world as fact'.* Carter asserts that fiction can do anything it wants to, more than we think it can. She proves that as satirist, fabulist, and feminist.

Notes

1   This and the above quotation are from Carter's essay 'Notes From the Front Line' in *On Gender and Writing*, ed M. Wandor, Pandora, 1983, pp 69–77.
2   Interview with F. Donnelly, 'A Room of One's Own', Radio 4, 6 May 1984.
3   'Notes From the Front Line'.
4   'Notes From the Front Line'.
5   Review in *The Guardian*, 17 September 1984.
6   For an excellent study of the female gothic, see Juliann Fleenor, *The Female Gothic*, Canada: Eden Press, 1983.
7   Carter told me she read a great many books about the circus before beginning to write. She particularly liked Masefield's *Memoirs of a Midget*.
8   Review in *The Guardian*, 17 October 1985.
9   Review by Sue Roe in *The Literary Review*, October 1981, Vol 2 no 41.
10   Review in *The Guardian*, 17 October 1985.
11   This and the above two quotations are from an interview with John Haffenden in *The Literary Review*, November 1984, pp 34–8.

3
Wandor, Rubens, Feinstein: Jewish Women Writing in Britain

A Brief Introduction to Jewish Novelists in the US and Britain

The large Jewish community in North America has frequently transformed the novel, with the inventions of Saul Bellow, Bernard Malamud, Philip Roth, Isaac Bashevis Singer, among many others; while Arthur Miller and Neil Simon have created contemporary forms of tragedy and comedy.

Their remarkable body of fiction appeals to a wide audience, because so many Americans are first or second generation immigrants, and often share their European past, or liberation from a class system. Jewish writers are not afraid to represent characters discussing ideas, or to exploit new approaches.

Each novelist in North America seems to re-invent the novel. Saul Bellow looks at good and evil as inalienable, like Dostoyevsky. He brings in the ebullient life of Chicago, with its underworld, its crime, its continuing destructiveness. Philip Roth plays with Jewish stereotypes such as the possessive mother, the oversexed hero, creating new structures out of his psychological conflicts. The Jewish hero is often stereotyped as neurotic and erotic, preoccupied with his family's demands, his gentile lover, and his analyst. These preoccupations are skilfully parodied in Woody Allen's films.

A central dynamic in the Jewish novel arises from the tension between the pursuit of the imagination and the need for a moral purpose. Comic contradiction is created by representing the Jew as sufferer while he lives in an affluent suburb. The advantage of Jewishness for an American, as opposed to an English writer, is that it can be used as a metaphor satirising contradictions of contemporary urban life.

For brevity, the following comments contain generalisations, for which I apologise. Novelists in Britain have not formed a cohesive

Jewish group, inhibited in a society with long established norms. However the situation of not being wholly acceptable can give a necessary perspective. Jewish writers working in Britain share a culture, but not a history. This enables them to see when British fear of 'solemnity' undermines serious discussion of ideas. What Jewish (and many Irish) writers bring is a combination of real seriousness and humour, whimsy and self-mocking alongside committed discussion of real problems through fiction.

The Holocaust casts a stronger shadow on Jewish writers than on British ones, though awareness of that evil is in the background of much great writing today. The need to survive the horrifying behaviour of fellow men has shaped Jewish personality – and writing. Such necessity links them with black women writers and their tradition of survival in the face of inhumanity. In Jewish and black novels the figure of the survivor occurs more than in British fiction, which seems effete or over-confident in comparison.

There is a wealth of Jewish talent in music, psychology, philosophy, theatre, film and painting. It is invidious to select only three women writers, but lack of space has enforced it. I have chosen Bernice Rubens, a fine novelist, winner of the Booker prize; Michelene Wandor, poet, playwright, critic, writer of short stories and *On Gender and Writing* (1983); and Elaine Feinstein, novelist, poet and translator. Rubens, together with Arnold Wesker, Howard Jacobson and Frederick Raphael, represents those who write directly about Jewish experience. Wandor is less preoccupied with specifically Jewish topics, like the inventive playwrights Pinter, Shaffer and Stoppard. Their themes and structures are too various to be considered a group, but one feature that marks them is energy: energy in their forms and their output.

Michelene Wandor: Feminism and Jewish Tradition

Wandor is a feminist who 'felt reborn' with the Women's Liberation Movement in 1968. As a playwright she was excited by the new possibilities of women's alternative theatre as a forum for fresh ideas and approaches. Her *Carry on Understudies* examines the attributes of contemporary women playwrights and the many obstacles still in their way. Wandor also looks at the relationship of feminism and drama, and gender differences in play writing – an area where feminist theory is insightful and instructive. Her *Look Back in Gender* analyses sexuality and family in post-war British drama.[1]

Wandor's poetry takes subjects such as *Gardens of Eden* (1984) and contemplates them with wry feminist humour. She re-introduces the often forgotten figure of Lilith, Adam's first wife, who 'transgressed' by refusing to be submissive. This volume is a sequence of poems in which Adam's two wives retell their stories, and address each other, in a variety of voices, from questioning and ironic to intimate and colloquial:

Eve to Lilith

don't get me wrong –
I have nothing against
first wives

ok, so you laid him
first; that's merely
a fact of life
so you got to know
all his little habits, like
picking his nose
when he reads in bed

he didn't do that with you?
I see

I'm not jealous. I don't
believe in jealousy, and
what I don't believe in
doesn't hurt me. But tell me
honestly, what did you do to the poor man?
He's a nervous wreck.
He can't stand up to his boss, he has
pains in his side all the time –
I mean, something must have happened
to leave a man
so scarred.

He's told me how beautiful you were
The dark, dramatic type.

Usually he doesn't talk about you
but when we – well, long ago –

when – at night –
we – in the dark, always –
he used to call your name
at a certain moment.

It's none of my business
but you must have done
something very special
to make a man
remember you so

Lilith to Eve

I merely said 'no'.

That's when he gave me
his attention
for the first time [2]

Wandor is multifaceted, writing extensively for and about theatre, while dramatising a variety of novels for radio, television and stage. These include the five hour *The Wandering Jew* for the National Theatre in 1987, *Kipps* by H.G. Wells, which won a Sony Award, and a stream-of-consciousness version for radio of Jean Rhys' *Wide Sargasso Sea*. (This is an example of intertexuality, of a woman's text – *Jane Eyre* – speaking to Rhys, who in turn speaks to us today of female frustrations and longings.)

Wandor worked with a feminist collective (Zoë Fairbairns, Sara Maitland, Valerie Miner, and Michèle Roberts) ten years ago to produce *Tales I Tell My Mother*. It interweaves essays and short stories on aspects of women's lives and social preoccupations, 'in the absolute belief that there is a feminist genre. It still stands up as one of the most ambitious feminist fictional enterprises.'[3] The first part of their book deals with work and discrimination, the second with sexuality and politics, the third with myth, motherhood and men. Although each is skilfully distinct, Wandor writes 'We have been invisible, we said. We will be heard we will be seen ... Alongside the reconstruction of history is the use of existing language to document and express changes.' (*Tales I Tell My Mother*, p 9)

She also acknowledges 'that I'm part of a wide-flung Jewish tradition, but it seems separate. That Jewish part of me has been secluded from my mainstream interests.' Yet she experimented with Jewish topics in a recent collection of short stories *Guests in the Body* (1986), some of which mention possession by spirits such as a dybbuk. Here she breaks away from traditional English literary structures in a way reminiscent of Nobel prize-winner Singer, who writes in Yiddish. Wandor considers there are problems over 'readers and critics who still see Jewishness as signifying *other* and cannot absorb it. We cannot place ourselves in our literary world and this impoverishes us. There is less tension in our writing than in America, so we are not as creative.'

She is cautiously optimistic:

In the future young Anglo-Jewish writers may speak with a stronger voice. My generation is linked by a knowledge of our European past. Younger writers have shrugged that off and perhaps they should. They are less embarrassed at saying they are Jewish, so will be less afraid. Fear of offending makes for bad writing, courage opens interesting possibilities.[4]

Bernice Rubens and the Mainstream Jewish Novel

One of the best known Jewish women writers is Bernice Rubens. She was born in Wales in 1927, has published over fifteen books, and won the Booker Prize in 1970 for *The Elected Member*. This novel takes a wry look at Jewish precepts and their saddening effect on middle-class life in exile.

Her first four novels chronicled the difficulties of Jewish life in Britain. Insecurity deriving from pogroms was being slowly overcome, and Gentiles were invariably incommunicative. She states: 'I am concerned with communication, or non-communication as is more often the case, between people and families.' Her people suffer and give pain through the real love and respect they feel for one another. 'My first four novels were essentially on Jewish themes in a Jewish environment, for in that environment I felt secure.'[5]

Yet the Jewish environment can stifle its members, as she represents harrowingly in *The Elected Member*. The central character is Norman, who feels he is 'elected' to atone for sins before Jehovah. Rubens suggests that within any closed group, like a family, one member comes forward to expiate the sins of the others. Norman is broken by this burden, so takes drugs which give him terrifying hallucinations. His inept father and childlike sister cannot cope and have Norman committed to a mental hospital. No moral is drawn, but as in many an American novel, the suffering Jewish protagonist represents far more than himself, the anguish of all those who cannot blind themselves to pain.

The context is perhaps too Judaeo-Christian; Norman cries out, like Job, against the cruelty of Old Testament God: 'Your wrath. Your jealousy. Your expectation. Your omnipotence. Your mercy and pity. Your sheer bloody-mindedness.' It is 'a cry which many a member of the Chosen Race may have made in the post-Auschwitz era. This is the story of the Jewish people, except that even the darkest moments of Jewish history have been redeemed by Messianic hope. There is no such optimism in Rubens' work, though it is redeemed by a black humour, ghoulish and wryly Jewish.'⁶

Rubens' fifth novel *Sunday Best* (1980) is ghoulishly hilarious in its examination of transvestism. The plot is ironic: the protagonist allows himself to enjoy his aberration only on Sunday; one day after he puts on his drag and leaves home, he is accused of murdering – himself. The inventive structuring recalls Hitchcock. Her sixth novel *Go Tell the Lemming* (1973) is her bleakest. It represents a wife who is too understanding, destroyed by her very kindness and lack of aggression. She is in the tradition of undervalued nineteenth-century heroines, and is viewed with their searching insights into repressive patriarchy. The discourse, in contrast, is stark, angry, and at the same time cathartic.

Rubens has also worked as a teacher, and as a film director for the United Nations. She incorporates knowledge of this work into one of her most acute, witty, humane and well-structured novels, the undervalued *The Ponsonby Post* (1977).

This novel is set in Indonesia. Its strengths are Rubens' unusual understanding of Third World problems and her humorous discourse in the early chapters:

Djakarta, like most Third World capitals, is pock-marked with monuments, rude fingers aimed at the sky. Occasionally the monument honours a national hero, but in the ranks of patriotic devotion the turnover is very rapid. Often the hero has fallen from grace, and possibly too from the gallows, before his monument has been unveiled. To cover this contingency, monuments to human beings tend to be very high, so that the features, except from a helicopter, are quite unrecognisable, and the only item to be changed on the stone edifice is the legend, easily replaced by the name, rank and credits of the current favourite. (p 7)

Rubens' twelfth novel *The Brothers* (1983) represents four generations of Jewish survivors. It opens in nineteenth-century Russia, and
ends there today, underlining continuing Russian anti-Semitism. It
begins in a witty yet factual register, displaying her skill with
different openings:

> It must have been snowing. Whatever else we know about Czarist
> Russia, whatever events punctuated its history, we can be pretty
> sure it was snowing. Snow fell in almost every Tolstoy page, and
> Alexander Nevsky subdued the Teutonic knights in a celluloid
> battle on ice. (p 3)

Her Prologue states 'there is something disturbingly modern
about its story, something offensively topical, as if no lesson had
been learned from history at all. "In every generation each must go
forth again from Egypt." '

Rubens presents the recurring persecutions of a fictional Jewish
family, from the pogroms of Odessa, through Buchenwald, to
present-day psychiatric 'hospitals'. Her characters survive because
of their belief in the family, in their religion. The love passed from
father to son and from brother to brother binds the individuals,
helped by Jewish festivals and rituals, in spite of real divergences. In
each generation love unites while conflicts divide brother from
brother, as one marries a gentile, another decides to stay in Russia
rather than go to Israel.

The book ends:

> Perhaps, in each and every step from Odessa, the struggle for
> survival was only a long and gruelling rehearsal. For the real
> battle begins at home. 'We're ready now', the steward called. 'The
> bus is waiting to take you to the airport.' Thus Hans and
> Benjamin, of the sixth traceable Bindel generation, from
> Bessarabia to England, from England to Germany, and from
> Germany to Russia, entered the land of their forefathers, not of
> their bones but of their spirit. Jakob followed them. He recalled
> the old man who had led Aunt Sarah and himself to the graves of
> their past in Odessa. Living Judaism belongs to the Diaspora, he
> had said. Did survival too? Jakob wondered. He thought he heard
> the minstrel singing. (p 501)

The historical scope speaks for itself, due to skilful clarity of
register. Her ability to represent complex historical movements

simply is claimed by some feminists to be a feature of many under-rated women's novels since the eighteenth century. Her skill to enter the male psyche lends strength.

Rubens has also written a television play *Third Party* (1972), and was one of the first women to do so. She adapted her novel *I Sent a Letter to My Love* for the American stage, and it was subsequently made into a successful film with Simone Signoret, as was *Madame Sousatzka* in 1989. Fertile novels appear regularly: *Wakefield's Crusade* in 1985 and in 1987 *Our Father*. She has the ability to use her female and Jewish perceptions to produce novels of vast range yet concise writing.[7] Despite a few awkward moments, Rubens describes Jewish experiences of alienation and survival with humour and invention.

Elaine Feinstein and the Suffering of Eastern Europe

Elaine Feinstein brings recent Jewish history and emotions to English forms. She composes taut, feeling poetry which enriches her ambitious novels. Her first *The Circle* (1970) examines the guilt and longings of a working mother, with the approach of a Mrs Gaskell. Her second *The Amberstone Exit* (1972) represents a girl's fascination with a powerful male. Her most wide-ranging, *The Shadow Master* (1978), breaks from humanism to explore occult ideas, and religious mania.

Much of her writing, from the fourth novel *The Children of the Rose* (1976) onwards, is grounded in the experience of mass extermination. This horror, which her Russian-Jewish parentage has rooted deeply in her mind, provides her with a topic few British novelists have dared to tackle.

Feinstein succeeds in finding words (which many survivors could not) by examining the Holocaust through the lives of two individuals. The apparently female limitation of centering a plot on a couple's relationship proves to be a strength. In *The Border* (1984), her finest novel so far, the terrifying Europe of 1939 is seen through the reactions of one Jewish wife and her poet husband.

Although of Russian-Jewish extraction she was born and brought up in the north of England, a dual cultural heritage she appreciates. Feinstein studied English Literature at Cambridge where she learned to write a 'springy prose, good for essays'.* Realising she

* denotes author's interview with Elaine Feinstein, 8 February 1984.

had to find a voice, she turned to American not English poetry to liberate her.

After leaving Cambridge, Feinstein continued to write poetry. She also read for the Bar, worked for a publisher, and brought up three children. She has written nine novels and four volumes of poetry, and is responsible for translating and publicising the work of four Russian women poets, particularly Anna Akhmatova and Marina Tsvetayeva. Akhmatova is considered by many critics to be one of the great writers of the twentieth century. These Russian women describe the major cataclysms of Europe in verse that has inspired artists as different as Stravinsky and Ted Hughes, and has significantly influenced the range and flexibility of Feinstein's writing.

Feinstein did not publish any work until she was in her thirties. Her first novel, *The Circle*, analysed a working mother's intense love and anxiety for her children. It is her only 'domestic' subject, though expressed with 'the voice of poems': the first three chapters were published by a poetry magazine. An editor from Hutchinson read them and asked to publish the whole. 'I had apparently become a novelist without realising it.'*

Her favourite novel is her second, *The Amberstone Exit*. It is a close portrait of her father, an exceedingly hard-working, devout and affectionate man. He had the ability to make money, yet not to be daunted by the loss of it. 'He was unusually loving and permissive, which taught me to trust men.'*

At first her close friends were men 'because they had the interesting jobs'.* But now that women are more liberated Feinstein considers her female friends more supportive. 'Feminism has given the strength to re-define oneself as not being a failure', she comments.* Feinstein does not feel limited by man-made vocabulary, partly because twentieth-century poets have extended the range of expression of the emotions she describes; mainly because she had to break away from a Jewish working-class background, and liberating herself from those restraints gave her a sense of freedom. This was temporarily restricted by reading for the male-oriented Bar. For her, language is divided not by gender, but by science and poetry. She can, with effort, use the non-associative sequential vocabulary of science for discussion, but prefers 'the associative rhythms of poetry'.* One of her most poetic novels is *Children of the Rose* (1975), which deals with Jewish suffering against a background of violence, as does *The Border* (1984).

However, the range of her nine novels is eclectic in discourse and topic. She values her science-fiction novel, *The Ecstasy of Dr Miriam*

Garner (1976), where the heroine's visions are represented in subtle, half-mythical imagery.

Her most ambitious novel is *The Shadow Master* (1978) which is set in Turkey, where a new international, political religion is created – and ended with the exploding of a nuclear device. In a style ranging from gentle irony to black farce, it is a bizarre re-enactment of a seventeenth-century legend, and explores prejudice, brutality and the longing for apocalyptic change. Although not well known among the general public, the novel has drawn perceptive approbation from fellow-writers. Angela Carter has described it as the 'wittiest and most elegant of apocalypses, rich in meaning and suggestion'. Brian Aldiss judged it 'a great visionary novel ... it mingles carefully observed stretches of this world with surreal intimations from another.'

Children of the Rose

In 1975 Feinstein wrote *Children of the Rose*. Its title suggests a symbol of resurrection, and comes from an experience she shared with her heroine, Lalka: both visited a Jewish cemetery near Cracow, where the tombstones suggested longevity and peace to both of them. When Feinstein asked why there was a bare patch, with a single rose, she was told it was the mass grave of all the local Jews who had been rounded up and shot on the spot. 'The rose had flowered from a chance seed, out of so much death.'* Traditionally, the rose in literature has both erotic and mystic significance; Feinstein extends the image to suggest the possibility of rebirth after mass extermination.

Children of the Rose examines the impossibility of sloughing off the past for Jews whose relations died in camps or suffered as refugees. The central couple, Alex and Lalka, middle-aged and childless, agree to part because Alex wants more of Lalka than she feels she can safely give. He wishes to free himself from his successful money-making and retires to a half-ruined chateau in the South of France. The book opens as he surveys the rocky landscape which has a 'murderous history'. He cannot escape echoes of persecution even here, as medieval fanatics had murdered Jews on this spot; even here he is not wholly safe as terrorists may kidnap him for his money, the money that has bought him apparent calm. Feinstein displays a female talent for suggesting the political arena through the personal.

The story is not so much told as hinted at, with the allusiveness of modern French prose. Feinstein has learnt from Proust that the novelist cannot be omniscient: Lalka never fully understands Alex, nor herself. The slight plot hints at sex and violence, holds our interest like a thriller, yet is far less important than the characters' half-sentences about their emotions and fears.

Feinstein's intertextuality, her use of other writings, comes not from Jewish texts as much as her Jewish characters' memories of the past, of their parents' suffering, of mass suffering, which surface in waking hours and dreams: Tobias, the Jew who insists on forgetting his past, shares 'springs of spite' which lead people to kill. Feinstein insists 'we must face the fact that "springs of spite" continue, even after the horror of mass extermination.'*

Feinstein's poetic imagination enables her to encompass themes seldom previously explored in women's novels. Many women have felt constrained when writing about war – an arena which has long been considered an exclusively male preserve. But Feinstein possesses the ability to evoke the Front:

> All round were sodden fields, without any kind of hedging to break the wind or rain. The trench bulged inward but the slats were firm and they were told it was better than some, even if the rattles and thuds of the front line were clearly audible. (*The Survivors*, p 74)[8]

Her writing is able to carry considerable weight of character, setting, image and myth. Her language is deceptively simple, often musical, then suddenly staccato. Many of her sentences have the metre of poetry, and she works hard, 'honing away', trying to find 'words that sing'. In *Children of the Rose*, a sense of fluidity is created by the absence of punctuation between dialogue and narrative. Fay Weldon praises her 'sense of the elusive', in dealing with haunting myths. According to Feinstein it is the *myths* with which we have surrounded mass extermination that continue to destroy us; she believes that 'if we acknowledge myths we can survive.'*

The Survivors
The Survivors (1982) is about two Jewish families who escaped from Odessa to Liverpool. The novel's scope is ambitious as it follows the families from the First World War to the late sixties. The era of the vast nineteenth century saga is over; Feinstein has evolved an evocative style that hints at complex relationships and disruptive changes, and leaves the reader's imagination to fill in details. It is the different personalities of the novel's two patriarchs that

influence the next two generations, as they assimilate to English life.

Her opening is direct and punchy: 'Two families. Two ways of life. And one city, Liverpool, planted on marsh and meadow. A city made by Irish traders first, and then slavers and shipowners.' An unusual, half-journalistic, half-poetic brevity evokes the factual past, contrasted with the sad, menacing present of 'smashed-in windows and boarded shops'. Contrast between money and poverty runs through this examination of the Jewish experience, from the slums to partial integration with the middle classes. Feinstein takes us inside the houses of street-traders and businessmen, whose offspring enter the Gentile worlds of nursing, publishing, lecturing. They share experiences of Sabbath meals and synagogues, *and* those of the era; cousin Len is sent to the trenches; a friend has a back-street abortion; the Katz family greets the Russian Revolution with the same enthusiasm as left-wing workers, and also suffers from loss of work after the Great War.

The social scope is wide: each character is an individual, yet most have archetypal traits: the eldest daughter Dorothy demands independence and work; Len is the cheerful schemer; Rasil, the tough earth-mother; Ian, the clever, rich left-winger. They are studied with empathy and gentle irony, a combination that involves us in each character's loves and apprehensions, and sets them in the perspective of their times.

At first, Abram welcomes the Russian Revolution as God's will; the subsequent harassment of Jews in Leeds has the ironic effect of saving eldest son Harry from the war by fracturing his skull. Incidents such as the taunting of the clever son at school are briefly depicted, without bitterness, because this is the West where, in spite of some contempt, Jews can survive.

Jewish *and* Gentile experiences from the depression to the 1960s are touched on poetically and sociologically. Feinstein can convey the effects of a new decade on a couple:

The quarrel over religion dispersed, but Diana's preoccupations put a distance between them, and she continued to wonder uneasily about God ... and what to do if she had children. In that shocked, uneasy condition she was unprepared for the arrival of the sixties in Cambridge ... And they separated her from Jake even though, to the amusement of more sophisticated friends, they remained in love with one another. And faithful.

But the sixties suited Jake, just as Diana could find no place in them. He crossed the street to smoke pot with the students. (p 300)

Elements of nineteenth-century omniscience merge with indirect free style to incorporate internal and external aspects of a character's thoughts. The varied techniques aid the progress of the story, giving rapid insights into motive, as well as a sense of historicity.

As in *Children of the Rose* she stresses the importance of myth in the development of the psyche, 'though it is far less destructive on these survivors: the Katz family lived by legends. Not all of them lies.'* She links this need for myth with the political questions and intellectual background of the period, through adolescents' conversations: 'They spoke of H.G. Wells, whose recent comments after his visit to Russia had been hostile to the constant Jewish complaints of persecution. Dorothy was disposed to forgive him anything because he had written *Ann Veronica*.' (p 60) Feinstein explains her intentions clearly:

> *The Survivors* is based on the contrast between two sides of my being. Both these families are part of myself, in fact depict my grandparents. Perhaps the autobiographical element helped critics accept the saga, an anomaly in 1982. But Diana is not me. She is too arid and efficient. The style here had to be more masculine. The narrative is tougher, terser, as a long book must consider the reader. I wanted the dialogue to look familiar and to assess in one-line comments, like George Eliot. My novel *The Border* returns to a sense of flow.*

The Border

The Border (1984) is a hundred-page prose-poem on suffering. Its brevity demonstrates how much she has learned from short-story writing, and Russian poetry. The double suspense of a love story and escaping refugees unites the private and public horror of Nazi persecution. 'The enormities of the human psyche are in us all. The responsible writer must face up to this.'*

Feinstein faces these enormities through the psyches of a half-Jewish couple from Vienna. The persecution of the Jews has become this century's symbol of man's inhumanity to man. By limiting herself to two people, she involves the reader and illustrates the connections between large-scale political violence and individual sexual treachery. Against the background of corrupt power she touches on the possibility – or virtual impossibility – of personal redemption.

In previous novels Feinstein tended to write in cryptic dialogue. Here she has fashioned a form to overcome that drawback: a collage of diaries, letters, conversations and poems, the speaking voice *and* differing points of view.

Her central couple are the self-doubting poet Hans and his successful scientist wife, Inge. The title represents 'the border between Hans and Inge and their two worlds'*, and the border between suffering and insanity. It also symbolises the border between life and death – and the real frontier with the Spanish border town of Port-Bou where they take refuge.

Starkly summarised, the plot sounds violent; yet it eschews all melodrama to concentrate on the increasing love and misery of Inge. Feinstein understates the terror in order to involve the reader's imagination. Her characters cannot fully understand what is happening to their feelings, nor can the refugees grasp what Hitler intends. Historical cataclysms are incomprehensible to those caught up in them; so are the shifting allegiances of double agents, symbolised by the shadowy Kurt. Feinstein deliberately leaves Hans's death a mystery, like that of many fleeing Jews. She conveys their fragmented experience *and* the mythic quest of modern narrative. Her allusiveness gains historical justification here, because it mirrors the confusion of Europe in 1939.

The confusion is alleviated by imposing a narrative structure: the novel opens and closes in 1983 with the memories of the sole survivor, Inge, 'All sorrows can be borne if you put them in a story.' (p 1) Art – and time – afford a measure of sad understanding echoed by quotations throughout the novel from the Marxist mystic Walter Benjamin. His perceptions stress Jewish attitudes: 'Death is not punishment but atonement.' *The Border* begins with the Jewish New Year, and ends exactly ten days later, on the Day of Atonement. During this period, which structures the novel, Jews assess their lives and attempt to make atonement – an attempt at which this novel triumphantly succeeds.

Translating Tsvetayeva and Akhmatova

In her compelling translation of Marina Tsvetayeva's work, Feinstein has made accessible to the English-speaking reader a poet of stature. Tsvetayeva welcomed the Revolution, married an adolescent poet, fled into exile from Stalin with her husband and family – in fact shared many of the experiences and longings and the despair of her generation. This forcible sharing of political suffering gives her, and Akhmatova, experiences of few women poets in the West. These are welded into Tsvetayeva's poetry which has all the flexibility of surrealism:

The July wind now sweeps a way for   me
Look at my steps   following   nobody
Liberate me from the bonds of   day.
My friends, understand: I'm nothing but your dreams.
('Insomnia')[9]

With such images she transcends the ordinary, the mechanical.
Feinstein's translations use almost no rhyme, unlike the original: she
considers keeping the spirit and rhythms of the original more
important. Feinstein's versions are both accurate and as fiercely
alive as new poems.

Tsvetayeva did not facilely reject the ideals of the Revolution,
which made her unpopular with fellow exiles in Paris. This
increased her poverty and isolation as her only audience was
Russians living in exile, and she could not be published in her
Motherland.

Her intense love affairs all ended in rejection, searingly recorded
in 'Poem of the End':

you must bite out my roots to be rid of me
inhuman   godless
to throw me away like a thing, when there is
no thing I ever prized
in this empty world of things.
please say this bridge cannot
end
      as it ends.

Tsvetayeva's sense of rejection echoes that of many rejected dissi-
dent Russian writers. This poem was first translated literally (by the
Russian scholar Angela Livingstone) and then put into half-rhyming
quatrains by Feinstein, unusually direct and fierce. Feinstein has
discovered an original voice of remarkable subtlety and intense
exposure of the self, seldom expressed in English-language writing.

Feinstein has also been influenced by Anna Akhmatova.
Akhmatova felt impelled to write despite the knowledge that
writing could mean death. Government opposition to her writing
resulted in the imprisonment of her son for fourteen years in a
labour camp. She and many other writers suffered hardship and
fear of arrest: yet the themes of mass terror continued to be written
about, expressing the peculiarly vital power of literature under a
totalitarian regime. Akhmatova speaks of the women left behind,

waiting in queues at prison gates, numb with fear, grief and cold. She sought to express a woman's view at a revolutionary moment when some women thought that to be equal with men was to be like them. Deeply religious, she rejected the idea that desire is contrary to God's purpose and sought to reconcile the dual view of woman as whore and angel, to express as completely as possible the rich wholeness of woman. The lack of bitterness at the maleness of the political world is shared by Feinstein: 'We give away feeling at our peril. Enduring pain is better than not feeling pain at all.'*

Feinstein's Poetry

'You can move people more by poetry and its rhythms than by prose.'* In her early poems she pared rhythmical words to the minimum. The complexity of her poems has increased: she includes more images, but her images are, in critic Hugh Kenner's famous definition, 'what the words actually name'. She begins with her own emotions and experiences: "Marriage" opens 'Is there a new beginning when every/word had its ten years' weight ..?'[10] Her incisively conversational vocabulary carries hard-hitting knowledge. She stresses the contradictory nature of relationships with gentle irony: 'We have taken our shape from the damage we do one another, gently ...' She understands why couples stay together

> in fury
> we share, which keeps us, without
> resignation.

The ending contains bitter tenderness in the face of wider implications:

> this flesh we
> loving together it hurts to
> think of dying as we lie close.

'The reason I mention death in the background of most of my poems is because it is underlying us, making us want closeness. here I wanted to show how, in a long marriage, you know each other's weaknesses too well. This means you can help, but you also know where to hurt.'*

In 'City Calendar' she achieves the difficult feat of a narrative sequence. There are echoes of poets she admires: John Clare (to whose 'Shepherd's Calendar' she wrote a recent introduction); T.S.

Eliot ('Tonight, a November fever, white/eyes of light'); Gerard Manley Hopkins, in some of her spinning rhythms ('in birds' plume and knife pleats'); and Tsvetayeva's unusual syntax ('Free day unmarked   open').

Above all she has found her own voice in this unusual attempt to describe the reality of seasons for a city dweller. Emotions aroused by changing weather are interwoven with intimations of cycles repeating themselves, and underlying our eventual deaths. This is a woman looking at the city, imparting a new vision through what she knows.

She claims that poets 'prefer visual images as sight is the most powerful sense'. However, her images go further and evoke the *feeling* of summer: 'This two weeks' tyranny of sun is past ... Now the garden follows me into the house.' Ted Hughes read the poems in manuscript and wrote, 'She has a sinewy, tenacious way of penetrating and exploring the core of her subject that seems to me unique: her simple, clean language follows the track of the nerves.'

The language also follows the development of a relationship in Autumn:

I wanted to carry your
one muttered offer of sanctuary ... into the daily and
sporadic features of default
defeat! And yet I understand
the timeless darkness that
threatens.

The oncoming winter fuses with refusal of hope, while 'darkness' also suggests loss and death:

I can only give you   my December city
this sodium-lit terrace and cold rain
while night flows overhead, and black trees bend
in the flow.   The birds sit heavily alone.

She understands the reality of seasons *and* their symbolism for town dwellers. She ends 'City Calendar' on a note of unity and partial hope:

If we hold together now ...
even the copper husks in the garden will be green again;
will it be in time for us, my love, in time for us?

A Poetic Vision

In brief poetic novels Feinstein projects her vision of a world where violence and sensibility coexist. In *Survivors* she has transformed a 'felt autobiography' into a vast social novel. How does this compare to the outstanding *Earthly Powers* by Anthony Burgess, another panoramic view of twentieth-century life? There is less cruelty or variety of sexual experience than in Anthony Burgess, but equal ability to represent the ambience of the century's changing decades, and a more convincing evocation of the First World War. And Feinstein's title is truer to the experience of most English people than Burgess's eschatological vision of evil.

Feinstein's most recent novel *Mother's Girl* (1988) foregrounds the personal – a girl's search for the reality of her parents – against an increasingly conflictive Hungary in 1944. Adolescence in England, influenced by Cambridge ideas, is interwoven with memories of the past and a slow discovery that her father had to support her by gambling. Feinstein here chose the speaking voice of a sister talking to her sister, a remarkably direct device. It is her simplest discourse so far, the female recounting the intrusion of the political in the personal, a strength of many women's novels since their inception.

Feinstein wrote poetry, novels and short stories with a full-time job and three children. Before the Women's Liberation Movement she articulated one of its tenets in her longing to develop her potential as creator, in spite of the hardships involved. Feinstein is significant, and like many undervalued women writers, merits wider attention.

Notes

1   Wandor, *Carry on Understudies*, Methuen, 1981; *Look Back in Gender*, Methuen, 1986.
2   *Gardens of Eden*, Journeyman Press, 1984, pp 8–9.
3   Sara Maitland in a talk at the Institute of Contemporary Arts, February 1988. In a letter Wandor wrote 'It was to explore the relationships between women's experiences, feminism and fiction that we worked together. I didn't start from the neat conviction that there was such a thing as "feminist genre".' 28 September 1988.
4   This and the above quotation are from Kaleidoscope, BBC Radio 4, 5 February 1988.
5   *Contemporary Novelists*, New York: St Martins Press, 3rd ed, 1983, p 566.
6   *Contemporary Novelists*, p 566.

7 Bernice Rubens wrote to me on 30 September 1988 'My latest novel is just finished. It's called 'Kingdom Come' and is based on the life of Sabbatai Zui, a Turkish false messiah of the seventeenth century. I hope it is a mixture of *The Elected Member* and *Sunday Best*.'

8 Olivia Manning in her *Balkan Trilogy* (1960–1965) brilliantly uses her own life abroad to explore the effects of conflict on those involved. Susan Hill in *Strange Meeting* (1971) achieves an imaginative feat in evoking the trench life of the Great War. In fact women poets have written about both World Wars, while the autobiographies of Vera Brittain talk of the terrible suffering and mud in the trenches. Today younger women feel less constrained and Nicky Edwards has just written a skilful novel *Mud* (Women's Press, 1989) describing in detail the conditions at the Front in the First World War.

9 From *Selected Poems of Marina Tsvetayeva*, trans Elaine Feinstein, Hutchinson, 1971.

10 All following quotations from Feinstein's poems are in *Some Unease and Angels*, Hutchinson, 1982 (reprinted).

4

Black Women Novelists: An Introduction

Black women writers were unjustly neglected until the 1970s. Yet as novelists, poets and teachers they have made, and are making, a substantial contribution to literature – and to other black women. They employ most literary forms including the personal essay, the short story and literary criticism to re-examine their history and transform our thinking about black women's culture. Their foremothers are women such as novelist and anthropologist Zora Neale Hurston, and Jamaican Una Marson, whose writing had been 'casually pilloried and consigned to a sneering oblivion', in the words of Alice Walker. Now at last they are finding publishers, a wider public and the serious consideration they deserve.

African, American, British, Caribbean – all are evolving inventively different ways of creating fiction to translate and transcend their personal experience. Writing is the key to 'free the colonised mind, to unravelling centuries of lies and discover the essential black collective self'.[1] Though they are all distinctively individual they display some common approaches as a direct result of the social, economic and political experience they were obliged to share. Reference to their black history and culture is termed 'contextual' and refused by many structuralist critics. (This refusal to accept the validity of some black literary criticism stems in great part from structuralism's European, white, male-dominated and academic origins.) Nevertheless it is helpful in recording the conditions in which black writing was produced. They all come from communities with an invigorating tradition of story-telling which informs their structures and dialogue. Toni Cade Bambara states:

> Stories keep us alive. In the ships, in the camps, in the quarters, fields, prisons, on the road, on the run, in the throes, on the verge – the storyteller snatches us back from the edge. Our lives preserved. How it was, how it be. Passing it along in the relay. That is what I work to do: to produce stories that save our lives.[2]

Communities put pressure on women to conform to the few professions open to them – mother, whore or maid-of-all-work. Yet these black women novelists all courageously offer alternative images of black womanhood. They all depict black woman as creator; cooking, gardening, quilt-making, transforming the little allowed them into functional beauty. Like the British women novelists of the 1960s, for them motherhood is only restrictive when low value is placed on it. Their writing imparts new value to the struggles of black women, domestically, socially and aesthetically.

Their writing introduces us to the prodigious story-telling of their communities. It is the oral response of black culture, demanding the participation of the group. Stories are changed, improved in retelling, achieving a Homeric effect of seeing people from differing points of view. This ability to exploit a range of narrative elements helps to keep black community experience alive. History is guarded in the collective memory, and is used by these women to understand the place of the individual both in the group and in the wider world. They use literature to discover forms of black American reality, and their Afro-Caribbean roots. They present the tragicomedy of racial and human error with stylish energy.

This energy is shown by black male novelists, from Richard Wright and James Baldwin in America, to Chinua Achebe and Ngugi wa Thiong'o in Africa, and by many others. They dramatise the suffering of their race in language enriched by pulpit, folklore and street. Nevertheless the men did little to encourage their sisters. The Civil Rights and Black Power movements channelled energies into political activity, but seldom released women from sexism. 'Black male critics act as if they do not know that black women writers exist and are hampered, of course, by an inability to comprehend black women's experience in sexual as well as racial terms.'[3] In spite of its many achievements, the Black Power movement was so male-dominated that women were forced to formulate their own position. They suffered doubly from white as well as black sexism. Furthermore their writing was excluded by the first decade of feminist literary critics, such as Moers, Showalter and Spacks. When so marginalised, how were black women to reconcile their sex and their race in formulating their feminism?

Yet it was the Civil Rights movement which helped release the extraordinary inventiveness of these black women novelists. 'I began writing at the time of the Black Power movement and the slogan Black is Beautiful', stated Toni Morrison, 'to show what it's like to be me.'[4] Black women writers have played a heroic role in the struggle for equality and freedom, both in the US and in Africa. Indeed black literature has always been implicated in the freedom struggle. After the first few years of the Black Power movement women began to realise they were victims not only of racial injustice, but sexual arrogance. Barbara Smith observes, 'When black women discovered a political context that involved both race and gender, our literature made a quantum leap forward toward maturity and honesty.'[5]

Black literary criticism is emerging, giving status to the analysis of black women's culture. Criticism makes a body of literature recognisable, respectable. Before the advent of specifically feminist criticism, many women writers were neglected. It was only with the onset of the second decade of feminist literary criticism that North American feminists began to appreciate their black sisters. There is still no political movement to give power and support to those studying black women's experience. However their art is suggesting principles for the emerging body of black feminist literary criticism, based on a study of black texts, black history and black oral culture.

Black women have seized on the wide variety of forms which their oral traditions offered, from fact to phantasmagoria, to create new fiction. They had generally met with more obstacles than male writers, who had less housework to share when young and a greater chance of acquiring a place at university. Black girls were and still are likely to have less schooling and less literacy. Buchi Emecheta typifies the obstacles hampering a young woman: married at 17, she promptly produced children, and also supported her husband and growing family with her earnings. Maya Angelou had to support her first child at 16.

Not surprisingly a frequent theme is the frustration of the potentially creative woman finding no outlet, like Toni Morrison's *Sula* (1974). Sula's inner void is caused by her isolation, her restless incapacity to create a satisfying identity. She does not want to make children, she wants to make herself; even in love-making she only finds 'misery and the ability to feel deep sorrow' (*Sula*, p 122). She allows herself to die, whereas many of the other women, like her friend Nel, use their love in the way they use their sewing, to create warmth as 'the hem – the tuck and fold that hid his ravelling edges' (p 83). Yet to achieve this they need to be loved first, in order not to resemble the unhappy outcast in Morrison's *The Bluest Eye*, Pecola (sin) who is rejected by parents, community, and herself.

These writers create realistic and mythic structures out of their experience. They incorporate folklore, omens and music, adding metaphorical richness to their stories. Certain themes are common to all of them: community; sexuality versus sensuality; the relationship between change and pain; the ill-treatment of their bodies by the men they love; the thwarted female artist figure; the description of clothing as iconography. Thus in Alice Walker's *Meridian* (1976), Meridian's railroad dungarees symbolise her rejection of conventional expectations. Sula's bright clothes brand her as 'sinful' to her community, while ironically bringing it together in condemnation of her aspect and actions.

Both male and female black writers exploit the motif of the journey. However these motifs are differently used. The male journey is often political, a discovery of urban exploitation or a descent into the underworld, as in Ralph Ellison's brilliant *The Invisible Man* (1952). Black male writers are more concerned with confrontational black/white issues, the moral outrages committed by whites; whereas their sisters represent their community and the indirect effect of white brutality on black male behaviour in the home. The black female journey is above all personal and psychological – like the journeys in female Gothic novels. We see the women moving from victimisation to consciousness of their worth. Of course there is a political element, but it is inherent in the revaluing of their community; they too make the personal political. Morrison's journeys are bids for freedom, metaphorical flights, frustrated in *The Bluest Eye* but successful when adapting African folk myth, as in *Song of Solomon*.

The black women's new freedom and sense of worth made them realise that their personal experiences are of valid, political interest. They draw on their own lives, above all their lived bodily experience of exploitation. They often fictionalise their autobiographical material to affirm the value of their identity, which had been denied them until recently because of sexism and racism. Angelou calls her books autobiography, yet she shapes her life story into poetic novels, not beginning with her birth but with a song, and soon swinging to the collective suffering caused by cotton-picking.

Emecheta directly transposes her own life into Adah, the protagonist of *Second-Class Citizen*. The most inventive is Toni Morrison, since she juggles her stories on so many planes, the surreal, the mythic, the tragic, the phantasmagoric, in describing not just her own reactions, but those of her community.

Another common theme is the interplay of the individual and the community. The heroines often go on a journey, in search of wholeness, in search of identity. They return, to explore the ways of integrating self into a community. Unlike most black male writers, they seldom lose a sense of solidarity with both female friendships and maternal love.

They all acknowledge how much they owe their mothers, (aunts, grandmothers, surrogates), those 'poets in the kitchen' as Marshall calls them. It is the talk of their mothers which gave them their love of language, their ability to affirm self after the humiliations of the work day. Significantly, Alice Walker calls her recent collection of essays *In Search of Our Mothers' Gardens* (1983) in tribute to the creation of beauty in gardening, in cooking, in caring. Their mothers' outlet for creative energy was above all talk, as language was the main vehicle readily available to them. They made it an art-form in keeping with African tradition, a refuge from their social invisibility. They inspired their daughters with their expressive power, their metaphors, Biblical quotations, parables, homely sayings. Many of their phrases made words work double-time, stretching, shading, deepening meaning. Paule Marshall shows the Barbadian immigrants addressing each other as 'soully-gal', combining spirit and femaleness in one affectionate word.

Toni Morrison points out that in church the minister would expect them to respond, to participate. A characteristic of Black art is the ability to be

> both print and oral literature. It should try deliberately to make you feel something profoundly in the same way that a Black preacher requires his congregation to speak, to join him in the sermon, to stand up and to weep and to cry.[6]

The overworked cottonpickers gain solace from their participation in the service in *I Know Why The Caged Bird Sings*, while students are wholly involved in the preaching described by Emecheta in *Double Yoke*. In a similar way their books expect participation, involving the imagination of the reader. Morrison stresses, 'To make the story appear oral, meandering, effortless, spoken – to have the reader feel the narrator, to have the reader work with the author in the construction of the book – is what's important.'

Like white feminists, black women writers realise that their use of language can have political force:

> My writing corrects articulated prejudices, such as the abuse handed down to our language as 'illiterate and stupid'. Yet white discourse is heavily dependent on black dialogue. Ours has the

strength of fewer adverbs. This leaves more to the reader's imagination. Jazz still has that feeling.

The rhythms and the open-endedness of jazz, one of the greatest black art forms, resonate in black women's written discourse.

Their discourse was first caught in slave narratives, which Angelou studies because they were beautifully written. Women writers are looking back into their past to find nurturing traditions. When they praise the slave narrative they are turning humiliation into triumph. Many black art-forms are produced from collective suffering, like the 'Blues', articulated by great women artists, such as Bessie Smith and Billie Holliday. We are witnessing a revalorisation, a re-interpretation of the history and suffering of an entire people. The slave narrative has been transformed into the ancestor of today's black novel.

Maya Angelou: Writing for Her Life

Angelou's literary reputation rests mainly on her five volumes of memoirs. In writing autobiography, she claims she is choosing a quintessential black literary form. Under slavery the whole person was degraded, with nothing but thoughts as personal possessions. Therefore thoughts, words, became the means to self-identification. Autobiography not only affirms the subject, it bears witness, expressing public as well as private subjection. Angelou maintains that 'a good autobiographer seems to write about herself and is in fact writing about the temper of the times.' She claims originality for the form because no white writer

in the United States has chosen to use autobiography as the vehicle for his or her most serious work. So as a form it has few precedents. Having made that choice, I can't be less than honest about it. So I have to tell private things, first to remember them and then to so enchant myself that I'm back there in that time.[7]

The experiences of black American women remained largely ignored when many of the autobiographies were by men. However 1970 saw the publication of some outstanding books by black women which were to reassess and repossess identity: *The Bluest Eye* by Toni Morrison and *I Know Why the Caged Bird Sings* by Maya Angelou. The 1970s witnessed black women speaking for themselves, distancing themselves from the stereotypes of black Mammy or whore in black male writing, which denied their autonomy. They were at last revolting openly, through literature, against the attitudes and ideas which had kept them in servitude.

Angelou's autobiography is a powerful, authentic search for Afro-American womanhood. It is remarkable for its love and understanding when compared to the despair and anger in the great black male novelists, beginning with Richard Wright's *Native Son* in 1940. *Caged Bird* recounts her life from the age of three, in the deep South, to the age of sixteen when she abruptly enters adulthood with an illegitimate child. Her world was one of violent contrast: love, from brother, grandmother and mother, and humiliation and alienation from the white community. The contrasting experiences are told in the language of her people, with poetic phrases, snatches of song and moments of harshness. 'I love its rumblings and slashes of light. I accept the glory of stridencies and purrings, trumpetings and sombre sonorities', she wrote of her people's speech.[8]

This first volume of her autobiography charts the black girl's change from innocence to awareness, impeded by 'masculine prejudice, white illogical hatred and Black lack of power. If growing up is painful for the Southern Black girl, being aware of her displacement is the rust of the razor that threatens the throat.' (*Caged Bird*, p 3) This powerful, direct, physical image conveys the force with which Angelou indicts white society. At times her later, adult, reflections on racism mar the flow; however they challenge the authority of personal anecdote, and help maintain a balance between individual and community experience. This enables her both to take us movingly into the experience of black worship, and to suggest how black people subverted that institution to assist their community to withstand white cruelty. By the day she graduates, the girl has interiorised her ideology, linking it with her description: 'It was brutal to be young and already trained to sit quietly and listen to charges brought against my color [by the speaker at graduation day].' (p 153)

One of her aims is the rejection of a sense of nothingness. A further aim is to examine her own community with honesty. This inclusion of internal as well as external analysis marks the black women writers. They have been unjustly accused by black males of unfairness, though there is no bitterness in the depiction of the brutality sometimes meted out by their menfolk. Even the weak man who rapes her is drawn with compassion and objectivity. He had been emasculated and undervalued by society. (However in a radio interview recently with psychologist Anthony Clare, she admitted that the rape makes her frightened of relationships, even today. In her published work she is less critical of the black male.) Most black women are reluctant to criticise black men in a racist society.

Angelou's autobiography resembles fiction in its creative organisation of ideas and situations to make moral statements about society. In her second volume *Gather Together in My Name* (1985) we enter the fragmented and alienated lives of black urban ghettoes. She meets the dispossessed: prostitutes, drug addicts, victims of social and emotional upheaval, like herself. But her mother's strength and advice help her through: ' "people will take advantage of you if you let them ... If you haven't been trained at home to their liking tell them to get stepping." Here a whisper of delight crawled over her face. "Stepping. But not on you." ' (*Gather Together*, p 108)

Through women like her indomitable dancer mother, Angelou examines what it means to be a black woman. She avoids the stereotype of endurance in order to rejoice in the triumph of her mother as a person – and as beautiful, not only in the eyes of her children, but according to the standards set by white society. In snatches of poetry she evokes her as a 'hurricane in its perfect power. Or the climbing, falling colors of a rainbow' (*Caged Bird*, p 58). 'She supported us efficiently with humor and imagination, but no mercy ... "Sympathy" is next to "shit" in the dictionary, and I can't even read.' (p 201) Even her contacts with the underworld are celebrated. And her grandmother is not the archetype with round, smiling face, doing nothing but cooking. She is dependent on no one, proudly supporting her injured son, her two grandchildren, and often other members of the community because of her success as trading entrepreneur.

Angelou contributes new images of black women as self-reliant, controlling the environment. Through her writing she preserves the tenacious women she met, learning will and determination from their experiences. Her conclusion is that black women survive through force of intellect. No option she took lasted long – brothel, dancing, marriage, singing. But her writing testifies to the decision to make her own life, free. 'I made the decision to quit show business [She had sung successfully in *Porgy and Bess*] ... I would never again work to make people smile inanely and would take on the responsibility of making them think', she stated in *The Heart of a Woman*, (p 45). (This volume is considered by some critics to be her best, 'blending the individual and the collective, the witty and the wise'.)[9]

In 1981 she flew to Ghana to do research for a course on 'African Culture and Its Impact on the West', given at Wake Forest University where she accepted a professorship. She has written a book of narrative, free-verse poems that signals a new direction for her poetry. She undertakes strenuous tours, reading her poetry, singing spirituals and advocating her ideas. She believes that

> freedom and justice for a group of animals is a dream to work toward. But we have to work diligently and courageously to bring this thing into being. It is still in the mind. It will take hundreds of years, if not thousands. Courage is the most important virtue because without it you can't practise any of the other virtues with consistency.[10]

In her autobiography, Angelou effectively banishes several myths about black women – such as Mother Earth. She repositions herself in the universe allowing herself a choice, even offering herself as role model, implicitly. The self-construction of the 'I' is a demanding, complex literary process. There is the mature 'I' commenting on the child of dauntless women; there is the black 'I' representing the trials and humiliations of her community; and a totally new 'I', correcting the omissions in national history, offering new ways forward for women.

In interview Angelou stated:

> I am a feminist, I am black, I am a human being. Now those three things are circumstances, as you look at the forces behind them, over which I have no control. But I have to talk about what I see, what I see as a black woman. I have to speak with my own voice.[11]

Her own voice is audacious, occasionally uneven. One of the most skilful passages in *The Heart of a Woman* involves a conversation with women married to freedom fighters. Most of them are African, one is West Indian. Angelou forges a powerful common discourse with them, a rare occurrence, heralding a new movement in history, the possibility of a new bonding – of black women throughout the world, using a shared language.

Notes

1   Toni Cade Bambara in *Black Women Writers*, ed M. Evans, Pluto, 1985, p 42.
2   *Black Women Writers*, p 41.
3   B. Smith, 'Towards a Black Feminist Criticism' in *New Feminist Criticisms*, ed Showalter, Virago, 1986, p 168.
4   Interview with Paul Bailey, BBC Radio 3, 14 August 1982.
5   B. Smith, 'Towards a Black Feminist Criticism'.
6   This and the following quotation are from Tony Morrison's radio interview with P. Bailey cited above.
7   Interview with Olga Kenyon , May 1987.
8   Janet Todd, *Women Writers Talking*, New York: Holmes and Meier, 1983.
9   *Black Women Writers*, p 10.
10   *Women Writers Talking*, p 60.
11   Interview with Olga Kenyon, May 1987.

5

Alice Walker: The Colour is Purple

Alice Walker is one of the younger pathbreaking black women novelists to come to prominence in the 1980s. Already she has produced thirteen remarkable volumes of poetry and prose. She was born in 1944 in Georgia, 'halfway between misery and the sun'. The South has provided Walker with spiritual balance and an ideological base, *despite* racist domination through sharecropping (giving half the crops to the landlord) or by wage labour. A southern writer also inherits a 'trust in the community. We must give voice not only to centuries of bitterness and hate but also of neighbourly kindness and sustaining love.'[1]

Sustaining care came from her mother, who had married for love, running away from home to marry at 17. By the time she was 20 she had two children and was pregnant with a third.

> Five children later, I was born. And this is how I came to know my mother: she seemed a large soft, loving-eyed woman who was rarely impatient in our home. Her quick, violent temper was on view only a few times a year, when she battled with the white landlord who had the misfortune to suggest that her children did not need to go to school.[2]

Her mother laboured beside – not behind – her father in the fields. Their working day began early, before sunrise, and did not end till late at night. There was seldom a moment for either to rest: they were sharecroppers, working for harsh white landowners. Yet they both found time to talk to their children, and encourage their talents. Though her father cared a great deal for her, she talks of him as being 'two fathers' and for a long time felt so shut off from him that they were unable to speak to each other. Alice Walker pays particular tribute to her mother's creativity, to the garden she planted lovingly, and watered before going off to the fields. Her flowers and her quilts become a symbol of black women's creativity which found expression even in the hard daily work:

> She planted ambitious gardens, brilliant with colors, so original in
> design, so magnificent with life … I notice it is only when my
> mother is working in her flowers that she is radiant … Ordering
> the universe in the image of her personal conception of Beauty.[3]

Indeed Alice Walker claims that a black southern writer has not
an impoverished but a rich inheritance given by 'compassion for the
earth. The heat is so intense and one is so very thirsty, as one moves
across the dusty cotton fields, that one learns forever that water is
the essence of all life.'[4]

When she was eight Alice Walker lost one eye in a traumatic
accident. This led her to believe she was ugly and made her shy and
timid for years.

> It was from this period – from my solitary lonely position, the
> position of an outcast – that I began really to see people and
> things, really to notice relationships … I retreated into solitude,
> read stories and began to write.[5]

At college she read Nietzsche and Camus with enthusiasm, then
went to Africa. She returned 'healthy and brown and loaded down
with sculptures and orange fabric – and pregnant'. She knew her
mother and sisters would disapprove of abortion, so underwent the
operation virtually alone, except for a kind girl friend.

While recovering, she wrote poems obsessively, about loneliness,
about survival. 'Writing poems is my way of celebrating with the
world that I have not committed suicide the evening before.' She
slowly began to realise that if a community is to be supportive, it
must understand its past: 'I deliberately use what I've known. I
write to preserve our history, a history of dispossession. My great
great grandmother was a slave. She walked to freedom with two
babies on her hip. In memory of her I keep the name Walker.'[6]

Walker's Early Writing

Since her earliest poems, Walker has developed a respect for short
forms learned from Zen epigrams and Japanese haiku. Her poetry
displays stark honesty when examining myths. At 23 she wrote
against the romanticising of Africa:

A tall man
Without clothes
Beautiful
Like a statue
Up close
His eyes
Are running
Sores.
('Once', 1968)

She takes destructive concepts about black girls 'cooking their meals/sweeping their yards/washing their clothes/Dark and rotting/and wounded, wounded' and rewrites them in the same poem:

I am the woman: Dark
repaired, healed
Listening to you. I would give to the human race only hope.

These topics are further explored in *The Color Purple*.

Her first novel was published in 1970, the watershed year for black women writers. *The Third Life of Grange Copeland*, now in paperback, traces a family through three generations of subsistence farming for whites, linking social changes to personal change. Alice Walker stresses the relationship between the sharecropping system and the violence that men, women and children of the family inflicted on each other, while exploring the tension between the need for black people to assert love for one another and the need to express anger.

During her early years of short story writing Alice Walker learned from European and Afro-American traditions. She displays this in the two dedications of her first collection: *In Love and Trouble* (New York 1973). The opening quotation from Rilke's *Letters to a Young Poet* underlines the dichotomy she experiences between society and nature:

... People have (with the help of conventions) oriented all their solutions towards the ... easy; but it is clear that we must hold onto what is difficult; everything in nature grows and defines itself ... is characteristically and spontaneously itself, ... against all opposition.

The second quotation comes from the contemporary West African novel *The Concubine* by Elechi Amadi about the emotional state of a young girl, Ahurole, violently sobbing at the prospect of being married. These strikingly distinct traditions mirror the varied themes of these stories, which range from violent pain to triumphant portraits of Afro-American women, confronting their repressive cultures.

In all eleven stories, Walker's protagonists share certain essential characteristics: they are female, black, mainly southern. These characteristics cause their dilemmas even more than the actual, critical relationships they are involved in – to lover, mother, father, daughter, husband, woman, tradition, God, nature. The innovative black feminist critic Barbara Christian states:

> The words *southern black woman* as if they were a sort of verbal enchantment, evoke clusters of contradictory myths, images, stories, meanings according to different points of view. Who is a southern black woman? To a white man, those words might connote a mammy, a good looking wench, or Dilsey, as it did to Faulkner. To a white woman it might connote a servant, a rival, or a wise indefatigable adviser, as it did to Lillian Hellman. To a black man it might connote a charming, soft-spoken perhaps backward woman, or a religious fanatic and a vale of suffering, as it did to Richard Wright. But what does *being* a southern black woman mean to *her*?
>
> Focal to Walker's presentation is the point of view of the individual black southern girls or women who must act out their lives in the web of conventions that is the South – conventions that they may or may not believe in, may or may not feel at ease in, conventions that may or may not help them grow. And because societal conventions in the South have much to do with the conduct of relationships, they must experience and assess them.[7]

The Developing Writer

Alice Walker stresses:

> I believe in change: change personal and change in society. I have experienced a revolution (unfinished, without question, but one whose new order is everywhere on view) in the South. And I grew up – until I refused to go – in the Methodist church, which

taught me that Paul will sometimes change on the way to Damascus ... So Grange Copeland was expected to change. He was fortunate enough to be touched by love of something beyond himself. [His son] Brownfield did not change because he was not prepared to give his life for anything or to anything ... He could find nothing of value within himself ... To become what he hated was his inevitable destiny.[8]

This is also the destiny of the brutal stepfather in *The Color Purple* who has internalised the humiliating judgments of white men. His main relief is the humiliation of his wife. Walker studies hatred from the personal and social point of view, seeing it as corrupting the individual and as an element in capitalist alienation. Individuals are divided from each other until the women in her novels see the way to end this by talking, sharing, loving, finding non-exploiting work.

The Third Life of Grange Copeland covers several generations, and over half a century of growth and upheaval. It begins at the turn of this century and ends in the 1960s. The first draft, of which not a single line was used, began with Ruth as civil rights lawyer in Georgia going to rescue her father, Brownfield Copeland, from a drunken accident. In that first version both Ruth and her husband are lawyers committed to fighting for freedom for black people in the South. 'There was lots of love-making and courage in that version. But it was too recent, too superficial.'[9] Complete rewriting of a novel bears witness to the high standards Walker sets herself. It is significant that she makes Ruth more downtrodden, less successful in the published version.

In the novel, Walker introduces another male, in order to widen her exploration of sexuality: 'I brought in the grandfather, because I wanted to explore the relationship between parents and children, specifically between daughters and their fathers ... and I wanted to *learn* how it happens that the hatred a child can have for its parent becomes inflexible.'[10]

By the end of the novel this powerful, innovative topic leads to murder, a murder exorcising the hatred. 'To him the greatest value a person can attain is full humanity, which is a state of oneness with all things, and a willingness to die so that the best that has been produced can continue to live in someone else.'[11] Walker ends the novel: 'He rocked himself in his own arms to a final sleep.' Grange Copeland understood that man is alone, but had begun to glimpse what transforms Celie in *The Color Purple*, that God is oneself – and the world. Ruth is left to live on her own, saved by her grandfather, Grange.

Another theme she wanted to explore was

> the relationship between men and women, and why women are always condemned for doing what men do as an expression of their masculinity. Why are women so easily 'tramps' and 'traitors' when men are heroes for engaging in the same activity?'[12]

This question, which so many white women writers, such as Angela Carter, are examining, radicalises Walker's writing.

She heralds the new confidence of black women in foregrounding women's work as an image for hope. She makes the shared female work of quilt-making into a powerful symbol of solidarity, of the making of functional beauty out of bits left lying around. *In Search of Our Mothers' Gardens* (1983) points out that black women, denied other outlets, turned their energy into the creating of beautiful gardens, into cooking and above all sewing. Their spirituality was intense, a creative legacy to their daughters. Yet they laboured all day in the fields beside their men, like Walker's own mother.

> There was never a moment for her to sit down, undisturbed, to unravel her own private thoughts; never a time free from inter-ruption – by work or the noisy enquiries of her many children. And yet it is to my mother – and all our mothers who were not famous – that I went in search of the secret of what has fed that muzzled and often mutilated, but vibrant, creative spirit that the black woman has inherited and that pops out in wild and unlikely places to this day.[13]

In spite of black women's creativity, demonstrated by their gardens and their quilts, Walker claims that 'To be an artist and a black woman lowers our status in many respects rather than raises it: and yet artists we will be.'[14] She considers that black women writers were for years not taken as seriously as black male writers. This was true until the 1980s, by which time her own work, and the writing of many others, such as Toni Cade Bambara, Margaret Walker, Mary Helen Washington, had achieved a higher profile for them. Through their art, and activist participation in the Civil Rights movement, they have all improved the image of black women.

Alice Walker has also worked as editor for a feminist journal, but distances herself, like most black writers, from white feminists because they fear 'knowing that black women want the best for their children. Better then to deny that the black woman has a vagina. Is a woman.'[15] In *The Color Purple* Celie finds her babies taken away at birth; like the slave mothers in Morrison's *Beloved* the longing to know how her stolen children develop, far away, is yet another factor in her suffering. This reveals the difficulty of dealing with the memory of the time when black women had their children sold off by whites, so making solidarity with white women, even feminists, difficult. Alice Walker prefers to call herself a 'womanist'.

Her definition of a womanist is a woman who

appreciates and prefers women's culture, women's emotional flexibility (values tears as counterbalance of laughter), and women's strength. Wanting to know more and in greater depth than is considered 'good' for one. A black feminist. Womanist is to feminist as purple to lavender.[16]

The Color Purple

Her womanism is most marked in the novel that brought her fame, a film and the Pulitzer prize: *The Color Purple* (1983). She exploits the one form of writing traditionally allowed to women – letters. Letters represent the speaking voice; they impart information about the external world and about internal development. Letters to God recount the touching, harrowing story of Celie, raped at fourteen and married off to a lazy bully, to rear his children. The emphasis on women's experience as they succeed in liberating themselves from male dominance marks a further step in her 'womanism'. At the beginning the girl is so alone she can only address her letters to God. As her relationships with women develop she learns to value the godhead in herself, to become a full person.

Religion and letter-writing, two of the very few outlets open to women, are used, as in the early women's novels of the eighteenth century, to find self-expression. Both then and now, the novel analyses the emotions of women to give them meaning, fulfilling a social alongside a personal need.

In a recent television programme, Walker stated:

I wanted to memorialise women like my step-grandmother, Rachel, I wanted to liberate that person. She was so battered down that her real personality died with her. She had to call my grandfather 'Mr'. She came to seven children, her own two babies already dead. She came to fields to dig, she came to smallpox, whooping cough; she came to death. And my grandfather merely called her '(w)oman'.[17]

Rachel has been transposed into Celie, whose letters describe the abuse of a girl's body, her lonely pregnancies, the removing of her children, the humiliations felt because deprived of love, respect, even decent clothes. It is through Shug, her husband's mistress that she learns to accept her kinky hair and short dark body: 'My heart must be young and fresh though, it feel like it blooming blood.' (*The Color*, p 220) This revaluing of herself, her body, is achieved by lesbian love from Shug, the only person to love her apart from her sister. Walker is prepared, like Morrison, to approach hitherto forbidden topics in order to underline the liberating power of the love of black women – the note on which these letters end:

Dear God, Thank you for bringing my sister Nettie and our children home... Us totter toward one another like us use to do when us was babies. Then us feel so weak when us touch, us knock each other down ... I don't think us feel old at all ... Amen. (*The Color*, pp 242–4)

Writing *The Color Purple*

In an article entitled 'Writing *The Color Purple*' Walker states that the germ of *The Color Purple* was a conversation about two women who 'felt married to the same man. I also knew it would be a historical novel.'[18] She represents the reality of the black sharecroppers' economic exploitation in the 1930s which her parents had undergone. Like Toni Morrison, she includes verifiable historical fact – in order to record the past of her community. Arthur Haley also attempted this in *Roots* but without acknowledging his debt to Margaret Walker, from whose writings many of his ideas sprang. Those with little knowledge of black writing may not be aware of its intertextuality; of how many black writers are influenced by earlier black writers unacknowledged or forgotten. Alice Walker stresses her debts to black women writers of the past, to prove that there is a living tradition, and to offer models, 'simply because models in art, in behaviour, in growth of spirit and intellect even if rejected, enrich and enlarge one's view of existence.'[19]

Alice Walker's approach testifies to the spirituality she witnessed in her mother (and many other black women) and which she has inherited.

When I was sure the characters of my new novel were trying to form, to speak through me, I made plans to leave New York, a place which the people in *The Color Purple* refused to visit. I was sure they were country people. Eventually we found a place in North California which we could afford and my characters liked. Seeing the sheep and goats Celie began, haltingly, to speak ... There were days, even months, when nothing happened. I worked on my quilt while Celie and Shug and Albert were getting to know each other.[20]

Similar spirituality surfaces in writers as different as Keri Hulme, who hears Maori ancestors speaking through her, and P.D. James the crime writer who talks of 'getting in touch with my characters – or letting them get in touch with me. It is a process of revelation as much as creation.'[21] Iris Murdoch points out how intense the spirituality of women saints and mystics has been. Both she and Doris Lessing are taking an increasing interest in mystic writings of the East. A feature of female novels of the 1980s has been a renewed respect for the life and power of the spirit.[22]

Walker expresses serious respect for those who admit there may be other human spirits in the cosmos – which is why she allowed Steven Spielberg to make the film of her book.[23] At the end she amusingly refers to herself as 'AUTHOR AND MEDIUM'. The opening dedication is 'To the Spirit: Without whose assistance Neither this book Nor I would have been written'. Walker here deliberately shares what she praises in black women:

spirituality so intense, so deep, so unconscious that they were unaware of the richness they held. They stumbled blindly through their lives: creatures so abused and mutilated in body, so dimmed and confused by pain, that they considered themselves unworthy, even of hope.[24]

We see here the Celie of the early letters, abused sexually, deprived of affection, respect, decent clothes, conversation, and apparently hope. Yet from this beginning, which encapsulates the lives of many nineteenth-century black women, Celie is allowed to rise, to find love, a fulfilling self-image and creative work, a new family, respect from her community.

In order to make this transformation believable, Walker has taken stereotypes, and shown where they should not be used to marginalise. Fay Weldon has said that in *Praxis* she had deliberately taken the words used to denigrate women such as whore, adulteress, castrator, murderess, to show WHY her protagonist was all these things – and not wicked.[25] Alice Walker writes: 'Black women are called in the folklore that so aptly identifies one's status in society "the *mule* of the world", because we have been handed the burdens that everyone else refused to carry.'[26] Celie carries this burden so well that she makes a home for her stepchildren while refusing to accept that their disrespectful behaviour is legitimate. She later channels her capacity for long hours of toil into the sewing of trousers, to support herself, with dignity, away from exploitation. Her endurance yoked to her creativity, is rewritten as transforming, no longer humiliating.

The Language of *The Color Purple*

One of the elements in Celie's transformation lies in the use of her own words to reveal her worth; her straightforwardness hits us on the opening page: 'He never had a kine word to say to me. Just say You gonna do what your mammy wouldn't. First he put his thing up against my hip and sort of wiggle it around.' This apparent crudity reveals respect for truth – the truth of Celie's experience, the truth in her direct words. We note similar respect for truth in Sofia; even after she has been humiliated, after eleven years as virtual prisoner, she can state to the white girl she brought up: 'Kind feeling is all I have to offer you. I got my own troubles and when your baby grow up, he's gon be one of them ... all the coloured folks talking about loving everybody just ain't looked hard at what they thought they said.' (*The Color*, pp 225–6) Sofia's speech bears witness to the flexibility of this language, its capacity for analysis.

Yet, as Toni Morrison commented, this creative language was abused, called stupid.[27] She points out that when whites say 'naw' instead of 'no' this word is not misspelt. As occurs with some working-class dialogue in British novels, the spelling of different pronunciations can marginalise, and must then be fought. Walker fights it by adopting misspellings.

A distinction of black speech is not to need the many adverbs and adjectives with which white English writers so often qualify their statements. Another strength derives from the incorporating of biblical rhythms, which many black writers would all have heard in church, often the most important institution in the community. 'You come into the world with God. But only them that search for it inside find it. And sometimes it just manifest itself even if you not looking, or don't know what you looking for. Trouble do it for most folks.' (*The Color*, p 166)

Such statements, re-visioning what the godhead in all of us means, implicitly revalue black discourse by demonstrating its subtle arguments. And in this revaluation, through the spoken phrases of hitherto despised women, Walker gives her language the dignity, the status it deserves. She rebuts implicitly the criticism of the black worker Darlene: 'Darlene keep trying. Think how much better Shug feel with you educated. You say *us* where most folks say *we* she say, and peoples think you dumb.' (p 183) However Walker refutes this by triumphantly repeating *us* on the last page of the novel.

Metaphors in *The Color Purple*

The sparingly used metaphors stand out against the dramatic simplicity of Walker's discourse. Two key metaphors are those of colour and quilting. They stress black artistry and link disparate episodes with patterning structures.

The title represents a complex symbol: at first Celie has no decent garment, only *drab* castoffs; what she longs for is a sexy dress. When she is able to buy one, she chooses the bold, affirmative colour purple. The purple flowers in the field signify joy and freedom. In the Foreword Walker explicitly states that her womanism is to feminism what purple is to lavender: that black womanhood asserts strength and creativity.

When Celie inherits a house from her stepfather she decorates Shug's room in brilliant colour, symbolising her new economic choice and an intention of affirming her personality. When sewing trousers she selects materials and colours to suit diverse personalities. They bring beauty and colour into everyday design, for the use of friends and families.

The word 'coloured' had been used, like the word 'negro', to denigrate a whole race. Therefore the use of coloured metaphors signals a bold denial of humiliating associations. Morrison and Angelou both lovingly describe different shades of blackness; Walker makes the admired Shug very dark, and beautiful.

The symbol of quilt making links episodes and characters. It represents women coming together, sewing in sisterhood, as frequently quilt making was a group activity, for long winter evenings. Pieces discarded by others were used to make something new and beautiful. Alice Walker kept the quilt her mother made for her and still uses it 'for comfort'.

Quilt making begins the moment Celie has a few scraps of spare material and time, and wishes to make peace with her turbulent sister-in-law, Sofia: 'Let's make quilt pieces out of these messed up curtains, Sofia say. And I run git my pattern book. I sleeps like a baby now.' (p 39) Not only does the shared sewing bring peace to Celie, it helps the women make up. After this they no longer allow their men to divide them.

When Shug slowly recovers from her illness, Celie decides to sew for her, 'Shug gets out of bed, asks "How do you sew this damn thing?" I hand her the square I'm working on, start another one. She sew long crooked stiches, *remind me of that little crooked tune she sing'* (p 51), stressing the parallels between the two art forms allowed to women. Shug soon donates her old yellow dress: 'I call it Sister's Choice.' (p 53) This name, suddenly created by Celie, symbolises the emerging understanding and love which will help transform her from ugly to beautiful, in her own eyes and those of the world. Quilting transforms discarded pieces into beauty, as Walker's metaphors transform her message into art.

Women in the Work of Walker

Alice Walker's treatment of women can be compared to the re-visioning achieved by feminist literary criticism. They both provide new approaches to cultural history by showing the value of women's experience. Their alternative perspectives offer diverse definitions of female creativity and writing. Feminist theory has rediscovered and revalued women's contributions, and shown them to be more diverse and eclectic than had been assumed. Feminist critics and novelists testify to women's experience in modern history; they examine modes of entrapment, betrayal and exclusion, – and possible ways of circumventing them.

Feminist criticism and the feminist novel reveal both similarities and differences in women's lives. They examine what it means to be a woman in a patriarchal society. They all point out, implicitly in fiction, explicitly when theorising, that we are in a culture where thought is structured in terms of opposites. These polarities simplistically oppose features such as male-female, active-passive, rational-irrational. The second term is considered a negative or corrupt or undesirable version of the first and used to condemn or exclude women, as Derrida wrote in *Dissemination*.[28]

The American literary critics Gilbert and Gubar in *Madwoman in the Attic* (1979) were among the first to highlight similarities in women's stories. Todorov (and Russian formalist critics) have pointed out that there are fairly few stories in the world, which are re-worked by individuals. Thus Emecheta's autobiographical story, *Second-Class Citizen* (1974), and Celie's fictional one have elements of Cinderella, in their rise from exclusion to fulfilment; though of course in very distinct modes. Feminist critics examine the frequency of plots about women locked out of power, battling against constraint. They show how women novelists since the eighteenth century take similar stories and re-write them, sometimes providing alternative endings, or more active protagonists. Black novelists do this out of their particular experience of intense physical hardship and tend to close with a revaluing of their community. They take their women from virtual exclusion to integration, like Celie in *The Color Purple* and Angelou in her autobiographies.

'As Black women we have been poorly prepared to cherish what should matter most to us. Our models in literature and life have been, for the most part, devastating' Walker pointed out.[29] She has set herself the task of ending this by progressively improving the models in her own writing. The black woman as creator has appeared as motif throughout her poetry and short stories and by 1983 had become central. Mary Helen Washington maintains that Walker is an apologist as she 'speaks or writes in defence of a cause',[30] the cause being the liberation of black womanhood. The treatment has become both more polemical and more successfully fictionalised – a skilful interweaving of two often antithetical elements. Yet as her aims grow more complex and far-reaching, her discourse grows more exact, based on the vivid phrases of black female dialogue.

The struggle of black people to reclaim their identity and self-worth is depicted increasingly through the struggles of black women. Alice Walker is unusual in claiming that this struggle should be based on the female qualities of love and self-awareness. She was one of the few writers at the time of the Civil Rights movement who located the struggle within the self. In this she is asking if the psychological effect of racism is too great to overcome – a question also implicit in the work of outstanding black male novelists James Baldwin and Ralph Ellison.

Walker explores it through the guilt loaded on black women. Historically they accepted the load, as Celie did in the opening when she does not defend herself against her mother's cursing. Indeed Walker shows the women in *The Third Life of Grange Copeland* being used as punching bags by their men. The son, Brownfield, consumed all the women in his life, and terrorised them. He preyed on women sexually, hurt them on purpose – and they accepted. They accepted as they shouldered the guilt of centuries of black emasculation. Brownfield and his father blamed and beat their women because they dared not stand up (for fear of losing their jobs) to the white men who browbeat them. In Brownfield, Walker illustrates how black men interiorise the judgments of white men: when Brownfield's friends ask how he'd managed to marry a teacher, he replies, ' "Give this old black snake to her" ... rubbing himself indecently, "and then I beat her ass. Only way to treat a nigger woman." ' (p 56)

Women in *The Color Purple*

Shug

It is Shug's friendship which speeds Celie's growth. Shug follows one of the few professions open to black women: blues singer. The songs of Billie Holliday reveal many of the attitudes which kept black women down: 'That Ole Devil Called Love', 'Lover Man (Oh Where Can You Be)', 'Don't Explain', 'Good Morning Heartache', 'There is no Greater Love', 'Somebody's on My Mind'. Shug throws herself into singing, dancing and dressing for the part. But she does not allow herself to be exploited, used and thrown away as happened to Billie Holliday and many others.

She buys a large house, keeps it, tells Albert his shortcomings, shrugs at her husband's faithlessness and admits that her lover of nineteen may only last six months. Shug is not only safeguarding her money, she safeguards her selfhood, with methods similar to those used in psychotherapeutic counselling today: assertiveness and levelling. She asserts her own value and that of Celie, and she tells the men, as equals, what she thinks of their weaknesses. Her realistic acceptance that sexual love may not last is counterbalanced by a valuing of women's friendship – which leads Celie to value herself.

Shug's self-respect is not unlike that of Angelou's mother, also an extremely attractive singer and dancer in nightclubs. Furthermore both these women display a wisdom learned in their working lives. Both teach the girl they love not to allow others to use or revile their individuality. Their punchy speech conveys centuries of hard lessons: 'You somebody to Nettie. Hard to be Christ but he manage. He knowed the fools he was dealing with ... Nobody feels better for killing ... Lets make you some pants.' (pp 122–4) Shug's brainwave releases the latent creativity in Celie, as does her physical embrace.

For the first time a black lesbian relationship is represented as natural and liberating. Shug loves Celie's body and teaches her where to feel sexual pleasure, a pleasure which Mr — never gives his wife. Yet it is the tenderness, the hugs, the sharing which are even more supportive than sex to this deprived girl. Through fiction, and resistance to cultural taboos in the form of Shug, Walker has given her humiliated stepgrandmother a fuller life than that of mere "oman' to which her husband and society had relegated her.

Celie

Celie is the heroine triumphantly rescued from humiliations to gain personal, social and sexual vindication. In the first few pages she seems to write to God, but is she perhaps speaking to us, to anyone who will listen? Her voice speaks first from agonising isolation, faced with male destruction of her mind, her body and her progeny:

> dear God, He act like he can't stand me no more. Say I'm evil an always up to no good. He took my other little baby, a boy this time. But I don't think he kilt it. I thing he sold it to a man an his wife over Monticello. I got breasts full of milk running down myself. He say Why dont you look decent? Put on something. But what I'm sposed to put on? I dont have nothing. (p 5)

Celie suffers like the slave women described by Morrison in *Beloved*,[31] who are not allowed to continue breastfeeding their children. Unschooled, renamed by white owners, they were seldom able to trace their offspring. Morrison represents the agony this causes, by bringing back the beloved baby as a ghost, tormenting her mother. Walker is kinder in her fiction, restoring Celie's lost children who have been brought up alongside the beloved missionary sister, Nettie. They are lively, intelligent and affectionate, so allaying the fear of social taboos produced by possible incest. (Though it turns out that the man was Celie's step-father and not a blood relative, Walker is making an important point about not accepting racist judgments which automatically assume that black men will sexually abuse their children.)

Celie redeems herself by her capacity to love. First she can only love her sister Nettie, to whom she is so devoted that she saves and scrapes to send her to school. She tries to learn from her even when she is tired, and then makes her leave to escape the rape and childbirth which marred Celie's own adolescence. Nettie profits from her education, returning as much love as she received, transmitted through her long informative letters about life in Africa. It is their commitment to each other which helps them mature.

Sisterhood is now a worldwide ideal. It has taken nearly two centuries since the French Revolution for sisterhood to convey a solidarity as strong as 'fraternité' or brotherhood – which too often excluded women.

The word sisterhood has of course been stressed by feminists. It brings notions of equality and love – as does trade unionist use of 'brother'. In *The Color Purple* the word is far more than symbolic. Celie and Nettie really are sisters. They help each other grow and share the desire to mother the bastard children. Their letters to each other validate their existence, develop their capacity to share, to communicate, to put their most important experiences and ideas into words. Nettie gradually takes the place of an imagined God, and helps overcome Celie's isolation. These sisters represent the new sense of solidarity which gives women the support they so much need in overcoming the divisiveness created by male power.

The seeds already existed in black female relationships as depicted in *The Color Purple*. When Sofia is taken to prison the other women automatically help with her children. And when Squeak decides she must try to make a success of her singing voice, it is Sofia who looks after *her* children. The traditional extended family, which can be such a burden, as it was to poor Celie when she married a man with five repellent children, slowly becomes bearable. partly because the new sense of sisterhood enables the women to accept each other instead of fighting. Celie is even caring enough to say to Squeak, Harpo's mistress, after his wife Sofia is taken to jail, 'Make Harpo call you by you real name, then maybe he see you even when he trouble' (p 75).

The black family had not been allowed to exist on slave plantations. (The protagonist in *Beloved* was not permitted a marriage ceremony.) The role of the father as supporter was destroyed whenever the man was sold to another owner – as often occurred. Women were sent straight back to work in the fields after childbirth, while only one wet nurse suckled all the babies till they were old enough to sell. Yet in *The Color Purple* we are given a strong sense of family. Not the nuclear family, but devotion to mother, to sister, to the idea of gathering together in a homestead – which Celie makes increasingly welcoming and warm, a base for all to come back to when the world or their relationships treat them badly. Celie symbolises the black homemaker who overcomes the destructive privations of capitalism to offer an alternative model – of family life as community.

Nettie and Africa

It is through Nettie's analytical letters that we learn about the wider world of Africa. She represents a working woman with a profession, though an unusual one – a missionary. This profession takes her on a journey which many grandchildren of ex-slaves are now taking: to find what Africa signifies today. Her work gives her virtual equality in the US church, but not in Africa, where she is perceived as a second wife rather than a worker in her own right. Walker's comments on Africa, in her prose and her poetry are searching and honest.

Through Nettie's voice we learn of the many problems of African villagers, and what Walker admired in Africa:

Over the mud walls I have hung Olinka platters and mats and pieces of tribal cloth. The Olinka are known for their beautiful cotton fabrics which they handweave and dye with berries, clay, indigo and tree bark. Some rush mats on the floor. It is all *colourful* and warm. (p 134–5)

Walker makes us aware of the physical hardships for many in the Third World:

For six months the heavens and winds abused the people of Olinka. Rain came down in spears, stabbing away at the mud of their walls. The wind was so fierce that it blew the rocks out of the walls and into the cooking pots … Children fell ill first, then their parents. Soon the village began to die. By the end of the rainy season, half the village was gone. (p 130)

She first represents the natural problems that frequently beset parts of Africa, followed by an account of how much the whites made the villagers suffer. They took over their land, without paying compensation, to build a road. The villagers were then even forced to pay for water, which had been their natural right. She uses this one example to sketch a brief history of colonisation. The effects of imperialism are explored as part of the process of de-mythologising. The only white missionary is an elderly woman who has done no harm to African beliefs as she respected them but is so full of herself as not to listen to her adopted African son.

Yet Walker does not condone the reactions of Africans to their dire situation. When they escape to the bush Nettie criticises their refusal to accept help for their children, while insisting on scarification (tribal face cutting) of girls' faces which makes them unmarriageable elsewhere.

Angelou and Walker find that it may be possible to make more of one's life as a woman in America. 'Though life in the United States is tough, the struggle can bring rewards', commented Angelou.[32] Angelou in fact (after three years in Ghana) and Nettie in fiction both return to North America. The fictional happy ending restores the two long-lost children to their mother – though we know the women will have to continue working hard. Yet we are in the language world of the novel where solutions can be provided, and reunions effected, after unhappiness.

Part of Nettie's function is to take us into a larger language world, to look at forms of exploitation in Africa. She analyses economic ill treatment. 'Children of eight and over are already workers in the fields. In order to pay rent for the barracks, taxes on the land, and to buy water and wood and food, everyone must work.' (p 205) Samuel is so appalled that he travels to England, to put the Olinka case before the bishop: 'Many of them are too old to move back into the forest. Many are sick. The women have small children.' (p 197) The white bishop does not even listen to these depredations, preoccupied by the fact that Samuel seems to be living with Nettie. The bishop symbolises white insensitivity, whereas Samuel displays the increasing caring for the marginalised which characterises black writers and missionaries who 'thought nothing of packing up for India, Africa, the Orient' (p 199).

Samuel's sympathy is wide enough to encompass the forced resettlement of American Indians – partly because he feels his wife Corrine might have Cherokee blood: 'the Cherokee Indians were forced to leave their homes, and walk, through the snow, to resettlement camps. A third of them died on the way ... [or] hid out as coloured people and eventually blended with us.' (p 199) Walker is interested in the fate of American Indians because it also forms part of the country's history. American Indians, like blacks, need to have their past remembered, a memorial to their suffering, and their culture. Walker is supplying this, by including fact in her fiction. Solzhenitsyn researches facts to memorialise the Gulag in Russia. Both demonstrate the power of fiction to record and explain experience. It is the novel today more than any other genre which explores our contemporary reality.

Men in *The Color Purple*

Walker presents a range of men, from the ideal Samuel to the violent, crass, irredeemable stepfather. The stepfather is irretrievably brutal, abusing Celie sexually and openly despising her. He feels no remorse, but turns his predatory eyes to the slightly more attractive younger sister Nettie. He gives no sexual pleasure in his frequent assaults, and finally, to get rid of Celie, gives her away to a violent lazy bully as husband. Till he died Celie did not even know that he was called Alphonso; he was a force, not a human being, to the violated girl. Celie discovers only from his will that he had made money, which she had never seen. He had bought property, apeing white capitalists and their meanness, like Macon Dead in Morrison's *Song of Solomon*. At least when he dies, his house is left to the girls. Celie's first thought is to refuse to live in it but Shug's reactions are sensible, unsentimental and realistic: see the cruel as they are, and accept that some good may come from evil – 'Don't be fool, Shug say. You got your own house now. That dog of a stepdaddy just a bad odor passing through.' (p 207)

Walker shows courage in not avoiding the topic of male brutality. Angelou and Morrison, aware of the racism of American society, are less trenchant, and recall a time when black men treated their women as equals, since all were equally exploited in the fields. Perhaps as she is younger, Walker can state publicly that there is no excuse for taking white racist violence into their homes.[33] She depicts their interiorisation of white values in the desire to humiliate. Celie's husband insists that he should be called 'Mr —' precisely because white males call him 'boy' and deny his manhood publicly. However, he is represented as improving slowly once the economic situation improves. Above all his women teach him to respect them: first Shug by being herself and refusing sexual, emotional and intellectual domination; then Celie by rejecting his view of herself, and teaching him, against his will, to respect her. Respect earns love and love allows the possibility of self-love, which he attempts movingly to express: 'I start to wonder why us need love. Why us black. Why us suffer ... I think us here to wonder ... The more I wonder, the more I love.' (p 239) This resembles psychotherapy in teaching that love and respect for self are needed for us to be able to love others.

Conclusion

Walker represents human beings painfully finding ways to save themselves by sharing their burdens. Her heroines vacillate between giving in to ill-treatment and standing up for their rights. They all show generosity in their suffering: some forgive their bullying menfolk, most are trusting, patient, even proud. Many display contradictory attitudes, yet they are prophetic in representing the potential of their community. At the end of *The Third Life of Grange Copeland* Walker shifts to the granddaughter to affirm possible futures, stolen from the brutalised generations of the past. That novel posits rural self-sufficiency as feasible. *The Color Purple* finally brings the work-place and living space together. Celie, sewing colourful trousers, represents an alternative economic basis for her community. This should not be read as cottage industry versus the alienation of wage labour, but as a socially imaginative female alternative. Black women writers can be seen as presenting a critical perspective on forms of oppression generated by capitalism.

Their female characters overcome almost insurmountable odds. They paint black women's resilience through images of their individual and communal achievements – the nurturing of flowers, of children, of female friendships, the transforming of shacks into homes.

Walker uses her skilfully crafted work to raise consciousness, not unlike the way black males politicised their fellows in the Civil Rights Movement. She expresses the commitment of fellow writers to her people, making the world revalue them. 'I am preoccupied with the spiritual survival, the survival *whole* of my people. But beyond that, I am committed to exploring the oppressions, the insanities, the loyalties, and the triumphs of black women.'[34]

Notes

1   Alice Walker, *In Search of Our Mothers' Gardens*, Women's Press, 1984, p 10.
2   *In Search of Our Mothers' Gardens*, p 238.
3   *In Search*, p 241.
4   *In Search*, p 21.
5   *In Search*, p 244.
6   *In Search*, p 252.
7   B. Christian, *Black Feminist Criticisms*, New York and Oxford: Pergamon Press, 1985, p 33.

8   *In Search*, p 252.
9   *In Search*, p 255.
10   *In Search*, p 256.
11   *In Search*, p 265.
12   *In Search*, p 256.
13   *In Search*, pp 238–9.
14   *In Search*, p 237.
15   A. Walker, 'One Child of One's Own' in *The Writer is Her Work*, ed Janet Sternburg, New York: W. W. Norton, 1980, pp 131–2.
16   *In Search*, foreword.
17   *Omnibus*, BBC2, 12 May 1986.
18   *In Search*, p 355.
19   *In Search*, p 4.
20   *In Search*, p 357.
21   See Olga Kenyon, *Women Writers Talk*, Oxford: Leonard Press, 1989.
22   For more on this topic, see Olga Kenyon, *Women Novelists Today*, Hemel Hempstead: Harvester, 1988.
23   Interview in *Charting the Journey*, ed S. Grewal, Sheba Press, 1988, p 102.
24   *In Search*, p 232.
25   Interview with Fay Weldon, see *Women Novelists Today*, Chapter 4, cited above.
26   *In Search*, p 237.
27   See Olga Kenyon ed, *Women Novelists Talking*, Hemel Hempstead: Harvester, 1990.
28   Jacques Derrida, *Dissemination*, trans B. Johnson, Athlone Press, 1991.
29   *In Search*, p 311.
30   M.H. Washington, 'An Essay on Alice Walker' in *Study of Black Bridges*, eds Bell, Parker and Guy-Shefthall, New York: Anchor Books, 1979.
31   Toni Morrison, *Beloved*, Chatto and Windus, 1987.
32   Interview with Maya Angelou, Anthony Clare, 'In the Psychiatrist's Chair', BBC Radio 4, May 1987.
33   *Omnibus*, BBC2, 12 May 1986.
34   John O'Brian, *Interviews with Black Writers*, New York: Liveright, 1973, p 192.

For more on *The Temple of My Familiar*, Walker's novel published in 1989, see review by Olga Kenyon in *The Scotsman*, 11 November 1989. These are two opening paragraphs:

The tone of her new novel *The Temple of My Familiar* is completely different, to be expected from such an adventurous, experimental writer. It ranges from the fabulous to the spiritual, as the title suggests. A 'temple' symbolises the spiritual part of the individual *and* our ancestors within us, while the word 'familiar' represents spirits both comfortable and possessing. These may not seem immediately inviting topics for a novel reader. But if you are prepared to accept her new fabular style of narration, you will discover a new form of magic realism which I shall name 'spiritual realism'.

We are given a new Gospel – according to Shug, the singer. She proclaims 'Helped are those who love and actively support the diversity of life; they shall be secure in their differentness'. This idea transforms the plotting, which is based on characters discovering their own diversity and facing pain by loving the diversity in other people, and the cosmos.

6

Toni Morrison: The Great American Novelist is a Black Woman

Toni Morrison was born in Lorain, Ohio in 1931. It is the scene for the haunted house and the snow storm in *Beloved* (1987), an outstanding novel of the 1980s. Lorain is a steel mill town on Lake Erie, where many black migrants worked in mills and mines once they lost their land as sharecroppers in the South. Life was tough financially until 1949 when her father achieved a measure of stability. She proved a 'bright' child and succeeded in gaining a place at Howard University, America's most distinguished black university. She hoped for brilliant conversation, but found that life for young women centred round clothes, parties and hunting for a husband.

Washington DC was at that time a segregated city. 'Thinking on it now I suppose I was backward, but I never longed for social integration with white people. For a place to pee when shopping, yes, but I was prey to the racism of my years in Lorain where the only truly interesting people to me were the black people.'[1] When enroled in a postgraduate course, she married a Jamaican architect, with whom she had two sons, Harold and Slade, now 26 and 22. The writing of her first novel, and her children, helped sustain her through a divorce. They

> provided the requirements I had not had since I left home. The children needed discipline, order, common sense, expertise, invention, constancy, affection, humour, truth, honesty, perception and a sense of reality ... When I veered toward romanticism they got constipated. When I got bitten by the world, they grew two perfect teeth.[1]

For the last four years she has taught at Yale, after some time in textbook publishing. Morrison uses little of her own life, except in *The Bluest Eye* (1970), her first novel, which she wrote over three years as she was working fulltime and bringing up the boys on her own. 'I was able to do it because of the history of Black women. I had seen people who had got through with much more courage than I ever mustered.'[2] *The Bluest Eye* was begun in the 1960s, the time of the Vietnam war and the Black Power movement.

There was this wonderful slogan 'Black is beautiful'. It bothered me a little as part of it means 'Black is pretty'. So I was writing about what beauty meant for us, for girls, for Black girls; I show how destructive that idea was. It's based on a real incident. A friend of mine told me, when we were twelve, that she had prayed every night for two years for blue eyes. She thought this showed God didn't exist. I looked at her and thought how beautiful she was. God is good and ignores us most of the time.[3]

She is less autobiographical, more inventive than Angelou, but just as community-oriented. In her essay 'Rootedness: The Ancestor as Foundation' Morrison points out the importance, for a black individual and for black literature, of ancestor-figures: 'timeless people, whose relationships are benevolent, instructive, and protective, and provide a certain kind of wisdom'.[4] In *Song of Solomon* (1977) Milkman's aunt Pilate embodies the ancestor figure. She had a dozen years of nurturing by two males – her father and her brother:

And that intimacy and support was in her and made her fierce and loving ... the best of that which is female and the best of that which is male, and that balance is disturbed if it is not nurtured, and if it is not counted on and if it is not reproduced. This is the disability we must guard against for the future – the female who reproduces the female who reproduces the female.[5]

This warning reveals close acquaintance with the debates in the 1960s about black family relationships. The Moynihan report blamed 'matriarchy' for black poverty! This stance of course absolves whites from blame, and fails to look at the economic circumstances which humiliated and alienated black men. In a recent interview Morrison pointed out that her grandfather, and Paul D. (hero of *Beloved*), both of them slaves, had treated their women with respect. The equality of oppression meted out on plantations, where men and women had to labour for long and gruelling hours side by side made them

fellow labourers in this serious, life-threatening business. My father's relationship was quite different from today, so friendly.

They had *all* sacrificed so much, accomplished so much, needed each other so much. All young men stood up in respect when my grandmother walked into a room. In the *absence* of other values you construct a world which is a little different. But when the village becomes a city it absorbs the conflicts of civilisation. Then gender difference emerges and spoils the comradeship.[6]

Such a warm analysis reveals a similarity to certain attitudes of Julia Kristeva, who insists that 'feminine' and 'masculine' attributes should not be assigned only to one gender. Black women distance themselves somewhat from white feminists because they feel they have been categorised as 'blacks', with little consideration of their femaleness. Indeed black slave women were agonisingly deprived of their children, thus their maternity. *Beloved* mentions the selling of small children, the sending of black women back to work after only two weeks' breast-feeding, forcing one black mother to act as wet nurse for a group. When Sethe was allowed to look after her own babies, for a brief time, she knew nothing about the traditional knowledge usually handed down from mother to daughter, such as when to wean. 'And whites could make a woman breast feed then beat her', observed Morrison,[3] amazingly unbitter; indeed the beating meted out to nine-month pregnant Sethe is conveyed in the image of a chokecherry tree: 'here's the trunk – it's red and split wide open, full of sap, and there's the parting for the branches. You got a mighty lot of branches.' (*Beloved*, p 79)

Even sympathetic white feminist literary critics may fail to appreciate Morrison's imaginative range and relevance. A review of *Sula* in 1973 in *The New York Times* stated:

> Toni Morrison is far too talented to remain only a marvellous recorder of the black side of American provincial life. She is going to have to address a riskier contemporary reality than this beautiful but nevertheless distanced novel if she is to transcend the unintentionally limiting classification 'black woman writer'.[7]

I admit with shame that white feminists are only just beginning to acknowledge how much they have omitted in their literary criticism. My work is an attempt to show the remarkable qualities of writers who are proud of their identity as both black and women in a racist, sexist world. Critics such as Cora Kaplan have made us well aware of the limitations of our perceptions; she demands that we read more of the black women writers and black polemics which were influential in the discussions and discourses of the late 1960s, when Toni Morrison and Alice Walker began to write.[8]

The form and language of Morrison's novels is not what white patriarchy expects:

> I am not interested in indulging myself in some private, closed exercise of my imagination that fulfils only the obligation of my personal dreams ... I write to keep history in our memory. Without ancestors you are dead ... If anything I do isn't about the village or the community or about you, then it is not about anything. The best art is political and you ought to be able to make it unquestionably political and irrevocably beautiful at the same time.[3]

This combination of political resonance and beauty is a feature of Latin American novelists also. They share the quest for identity in a society which devalues and humiliates the individual. So the individual calls on the rich culture of folk stories to give mythic significance to this quest. Gabriel Garcia Marquez did this spectacularly, winning the Nobel prize – while Morrison deserves a wider public. They both fuse real and mythic elements from their communities in an exhilarating combination of magic and realism. 'Here one loved knowing that at any time anyone might do anything. Not wilderness where there was system, or the logic of lions, trees, toads and birds, but wild wilderness where there was none.' (*Song of Solomon*, p. 138) At the end of that novel Milkman realises that he loved his aunt because 'without leaving the ground she could fly' (p 336). The black section of the town in *Sula* is a hillside called the Bottom; the valley is metaphorically the top since that is where whites live. This is a world decidedly askew, where reality is redefined to suit the wishes of the powerful.

In *Tar Baby* (1981) an African woman looks like a goddess with 'something in her eyes so powerful it had burnt away the eyelashes' (p 45). Morrison represents as part of black culture this

> acceptance of the supernatural and a profound rootedness in the real world, neither taking precedence over the other. We are a very practical people, very down-to-earth, even shrewd. But within that practicality we also accepted superstition and magic, which is another way of knowing things. To blend the two worlds together at the same time was enhancing, not limiting.[9]

The magic gives a quality both to experience and place. Indeed Morrison can be compared to Faulkner, in the creation of a place that is both mythical and real. Her Medallion is an apparently ordinary town yet supernatural events occur in its cultural matrix. Behind the ordinary streets are shacks where homebrewed wine nurtures traditions, and the black property speculator with the ironic name of Macon Dead spurns his fellows.

> Tired, irritable, he walked down Fifteenth Street, glancing up as he passed one of his other houses, its silhouette melting in the light that trembled between dusk and twilight. Scattered here and there, his houses stretched up beyond him like squat ghosts with hooded eyes, in league with one another to make him feel like an outsider, the propertyless, landless wanderer. (*Song of Solomon*, p 32)

Such Dickensian capacity to represent subconscious guilt through description of place demonstrates the superficiality of those critics who believe that the definition 'black woman writer' indicates a limitation of subject or readership.

Morrison's topics frequently reflect the 'universal', as she feels free to adapt both black folk tales and myths of world literature, such as the myth of Icarus, who attempted to fly on home-made wings. *Song of Solomon* opens with a desperate insurance agent promising to 'fly away on my own wings at 3 p.m.' The young protagonist, Milkman, journeys to the South in search of his ancestors. A children's playground song makes him realise he is descended from the great African Solomon, who was seen to fly (to escape from slavery). The novel ends with the daring spiritual discovery that 'If you surrendered to the air, you could ride it' (p 336). She renews the power of the myth by using it to examine how a black adolescent finds values to deal with contemporary problems.

Morrison's Language

Morrison is praised for her richness of language. Atwood calls her writing 'antiminimalist'.[10] Her writing displays the suggestiveness and paradoxical simplicity of black speech, the clear rhythms of the blues and the complexity of folktales. 'The adult pain rested somewhere under the eyelids, somewhere under their head rags, somewhere in the frayed lapels, somewhere in the sinews' curve.'

(*Sula*, p 12) Here the incantatory repetition transforms the prose into mournful, compassionate poetry.

Yet she can be startlingly direct when she wishes. The fewest necessary historical details are woven into the narrative on the opening page: 'Ohio had been calling itself a state only seventy years when first one brother then the next stuffed quilt packing into his hat and crept away.' (*Beloved*, p 3)

Her technique here is to leave out much of the background in order to start our imaginations working:

> It is the affective and participatory relationship between artist and audience that is of primary importance ... to have the reader work with the narrator in the construction of the book. What is left out is as important as what's there.[11]

She involves many strategies, from rhythms of black speech to white stream-of-consciousness. At times she includes both, to take us into her characters' thoughts: 'Why was there nothing it refused? No misery, no regret, no hateful picture too rotten to accept?', moans Sethe (p 70). The main themes of *Beloved* are the horror of remembering the unspeakable, the need to forget, the impossibility of freeing oneself from such a terrifying past. The characters' past tormenting their present is symbolised by Beloved, the baby girl ghost.

Morrison also manipulates irony and paradox in her examination of black values. She implicitly criticises the upwardly mobile who reject black qualities, such as Nel's parents who 'succeeded in rubbing down to a dull glow any sparkle or splutter she had'. The inadequacies of much human love are represented through grotesques, while the inadequacies of a community conclude her two first novels. (The Irish woman writer Flannery O'Connor, an outsider in the South, also represented the vulnerability of the rejected through her portrayals of grotesques.) The townspeople in *The Bluest Eye* achieve a false superiority by believing themselves superior to the ugly, impoverished heroine: 'We honed our egos on her, padded our characters with her frailty, and yawned in the fantasy of our strength.' Her intelligent, rhythmic writing inserts reservations into apparently direct description: 'We raised our children and reared our crops; we let infants grow and the property develop.' Such freshness of verbal nuance and rethinking of metaphor allow more than comment – she points the way to social change, delicately, undogmatically.

Morrison's Novels

The Bluest Eye

Her first novel *The Bluest Eye* (1970) explores the effect of community acceptance or rejection on the individual. A girl's need to be loved is doomed: raped by her father, rejected by her mother, she longs to escape but can only 'flail her arms like a bird in a grotesquely futile effort to fly' (p 52). Her personal fate represents the frustration of black girls' longing for 'blue eyes' – for an unattainable image.

Sula

Her second novel *Sula* (1973) is praised by black feminist Barbara Smith as bringing a new perspective: Smith sees the central friendship as lesbian in its closeness, compared to the inadequate heterosexual relationships represented, in the family and marriage.[12]

Morrison, like Alice Walker, courageously represents formerly taboo themes, such as lesbian love. But she makes them part of a much larger whole, where surreal and poetic events equal the 'real'. *Sula* displays Morrison's ability to conjure the reader into a suspension of disbelief. Sula's grandmother cuts off her leg to feed her children and sets fire to her drug-addicted son out of love. Sula cuts the tip off her finger to intimidate white boys who threaten her at school. These 'events' are woven into a study of intense loneliness, only relieved by the friendship between Sula and Nel:

> They were solitary little girls whose loneliness was so profound it intoxicated them and sent them stumbling into technicolored visions that always included a presence, a someone who, quite like the dreamer, shared the delight of the dream ... Because each had discovered years before that they were neither white nor male, and that all freedom and triumph was forbidden them, they had set about creating something else to be. Daughters of distant mothers and incomprehensible fathers, they found in each other's eyes the intimacy they were looking for. (p 52)

The support of female bonding, represented in the background in earlier black women's novels, becomes a paean by the late 1970s to the succour, the sense of redemption which women give each other in adversity.

Morrison's verbal magic takes us into the loneliness of soul of her central characters. When Nel's husband leaves she realises that she has to live 'with no thighs and no heart, just her brain raveling away' (p 108). When contact is made between lovers, it is lyrically represented. Sula imagines herself an artisan rubbing, scraping, chiseling to reveal the gold leaf beneath the black skin, then the alabaster beneath the gold. 'The reader is to come in', Morrison states, 'with his own sexuality, his or her own delight and work with me.'[3] She demands a sophisticated use of the reader's imagination, consciously seeking response.

Song of Solomon

This brilliantly written, half-magical spiritual quest for roots centres on an adolescent male as 'realistically' fleshed as her female heroines. Milkman, overindulged by his mother, first reveres the capitalist values of his unrelenting property-speculating father, Macon Dead, until he learns about white tyranny from his friend Guitar. Set in the 1960s, when black people, even black children were being lynched in the southern United States, the novel is enhanced with flashbacks to the thirties, through firsthand accounts of his father and aunt in the South. His aunt Pilate 'pilots' him by teaching him to value love, spontaneity and detachment from material goods. While journeying south, Milkman has to overcome archetypal challenges – the lure of gold, fear of others and fear of death – and to value the woman he has abandoned. Symbolically he is divested of his ego, and gains a new one. He is finally rewarded by a sense of bonding with Guitar, freedom from guilt and a sense of transcendence, the possibility of flight.[13]

Tar Baby

In *Song of Solomon* Morrison incorporated Afro-American stories of African slaves who 'flew home'. Her novel *Tar Baby* (1981) is set partly in Africa. It represents a greater variety of characters for whom the search is central, though unresolved. The beautiful black girl Jade had been brought up in Paris and learned more about white culture than her own. When she falls in love with rough rural Son they are both caught, like the legendary tar baby, and try to trap each other into their own brier patch. But their needs, desires, even dreams are at cross purposes. Son tries to

> manipulate her dreams, insert his own about yellow houses and
> black ladies in white dresses minding the pie table, and the sound
> of six-string guitar ... he barely had time to breathe into her the
> smell of tar ... he knew that at any moment she might talk back or

worse, press her dreams of gold and honey-colored silk into him and who would mind the pie table? (p 120)

Many characters are displaced, alienated from their cultures, fighting verbal and dream duels. Jade 'has lost her true and ancient properties' (p 304) which she might learn in Africa. Maya Angelou and Paule Marshall felt they had repossessed them when they stayed on that continent. Morrison indicts black as well as white for failing to respond sufficiently to individuals, and their origins. Like the other black women writers mentioned here, she represents mothers as unifying, nurturing, essential to the imagery and the message: Therese has 'magic breasts' which sustain. There is a continuum of theme but each novel is imaginatively specific. Her language imparts a moving, ironic, exquisitely fabulous vision of psychological motivation – of women especially, of black people particularly, and of the human generally.

Beloved

Beloved (1987) is Morrison's greatest novel so far. It is set just after the American Civil War, in the period of so-called Reconstruction. A great deal of random violence was meted out to blacks, including those freed by Emancipation and the few who had managed to buy their freedom earlier. Morrison includes flashbacks, painful but necessary 'rememorings' of their recent past as slaves, which indirectly cause the novel's bizarre and calamitous events. The setting is divided between the countryside near Cincinnati, where Morrison herself grew up, and the ironically-named plantation Sweet Home in Kentucky, from which they fled 18 years before. The central female character Sethe is based on the real woman Margaret Gardner who became

a *cause célèbre* in Cincinnati, because she tried to kill her children to prevent their being taken back into slavery with her, under the Fugitive Slave Law. Not that it was considered a crime to murder her children, she was tried for stealing property – herself. Her end was much worse than Sethe's because she was sent back to the slave owner whom she said she'd rather die than return to.[9]

There are other stories and voices, to widen the examination of slavery and its effects on the individual psyche. But Sethe is the central voice, a woman in her mid-thirties, who lives in an Ohio house, number 124, which 'was spiteful. Full of a baby's venom' we are told in the first sentence, thus preparing us for her dual registers of real and supernatural. This is a historical novel, and also a ghost story. The malicious, angry ghost is Sethe's baby daughter, whose throat was cut for love. Sethe had wanted 'Dearly Beloved' on the tombstone, but could only afford one word, to be paid for by having sex with the engraver. In that world of poverty and slavery, human beings are merchandise, everything has a price, and the price is tyrannical.

The supernatural element is not treated with horror, as in Edgar Allen Poe, but with 'magnificent practicality'[10] like the ghost of Catherine Earnshaw. As a child her parents told Morrison thrilling ghost stories, which had meaning, as for Shakespeare. 'I was pleased with the strategy of the ghost because it helps the reader understand the factually incredible thing which was slavery. The strategy helped me because you can play around with a ghost and you can take your time worrying about the dimension of magic.'[6] Morrison's comments are valuable, as she has put so much thought into the evolving of new forms for her new theme:

> It was a process of trying hard not to remember, and a process of letting memory seep in, while the images slowly come back. This type of memory slowly suggested the structure – and formed the way the process is revealed: now it's memory; now it's history; now it's the past we can't avoid. The ghost shows you must do something, you cannot avoid the past, you must collect it in some way. She is a manifestation of memory *and* a real survivor of the past which no one talks about – the slave ships. When she refers to survivors from those ships (like her own grandmother, who was raped then), her language is the same as those returned from the dead. *Yet* she has to be exorcised, chastised, got rid of, because no one who has to do with that memory is able to go on.[6]

In fact the white American male writers could not deal with this vast topic, although some suggest it with their symbolism of evil, destructiveness, nameless dread. A.S. Byatt considers

> it is an American masterpiece, and one which, moreover, in a curious way reassesses all the major novels of the time in which it is set. Melville, Hawthorne, Poe, wrote riddling allegories about the nature of evil, the haunting of unappeased spirits, the inverted opposition of blackness and whiteness. Toni Morrison

has with plainness and grace and terror – and judgment – solved the riddle, and shown us the world which haunted theirs.[14]

Morrison corrects many misrepresentations of black reactions to slavery. Though they were not allowed to form lasting families, they longed to do so, and the women achieve this for brief moments. Black men here show understanding, particularly the gentle Paul D. who comes back to Sethe and restores her self-confidence at the end of the novel. Their conversations are magnificent attempts at reaching through to another person. The only part of an individual name he possesses is D. (because all the men on the plantation were called Paul) so he knows 'for a used-to-be-slave women to love anything that much was dangerous, especially if it was her children she had settled on to love; the best was to love just a little bit' (p 14).

Morrison depicts black experience not only from the inside, but from the outside. She first shows us the mother killing her children, to free them from capture, through the eyes of the men who come to recapture her. In an interview, Morrison elaborates on this outlook:

> You have to look at it through the eyes of people who are shocked by it. I as narrator, as non-poking, non-threatening narrator, want to hold the reader's hand and say 'it's alright, you can go in here, I'll take you … so I have to move the camera around from place to place. You have to permit the reader to go through the horror as outsider before allowing or encouraging him or her to go through it as insider.[9]

Thus the most harrowing central incident, taken from history, the killing of children out of love, is tackled from this double perspective, first the white male's then only later the black mother's. Yet the cruel irony which forces Sethe to this act never diminishes our esteem for her in her misery. Indeed the incident symbolises the ghastly choices forced on all slaves including Jews in the Nazi concentration camps. Morrison has faced the same problem as those who write about the Holocaust: how to find words to represent such terrible experiences.

In order to reconstruct black experience, one of Morrison's many techniques is that of exclusion – exclusion of the Civil War and white people. 'The War would have been too central, it would have dissipated my energy from the inner life of those slaves.'[6] She is highly conscious of the techniques she needs to achieve her effects.

She cuts out many adverbs, as in black speech, because she can *hear* the way her people talk. She develops this technique of suggestion by eliminating most adjectives, deliberately, in order to invite the reader to use imagination. The spareness and concreteness of black speech is transformed into sophisticated discourse. By making the ghost girl represent the living memories of slaves, she stretches our imagination more than many contemporary novelists. For her the other world exists, magic works – and her prose achieves this. Her prose is a catalyst for revelation, and an exorcism – and a celebration of the 'giants and giantesses who survived', as she describes her grandparents and their relatives, all ex-slaves.[3]

The Language of *Beloved*

In *Beloved* Morrison shifts into poetry for a dialogue between mother Sethe and daughter Denver:

> I was going to help you but the clouds got in the way.
> There're no clouds here.
> If they put an iron circle round your neck I will bite it away.
> Beloved.
> I will make you a round basket.
> You're back. You're back. (*Beloved*, p 215)

This is 'quite deliberate' Morrison stated, a poem to dignify the conversation of black mothers with their children. Many of these mothers are given a directness which is, at the same time, simple, and intensely meaningful: 'I have other things to do: worry, for example about tomorrow, about Denver, about Beloved, about age and sickness, not to speak of love.' (p 70) This rethinking of their discourse endows them with a dignity, not given by the great black male novelists Ellison and Wright. Her shift into poetry recalls the blues, their distillation of feeling: 'It was music that carried us.'[1] But Morrison points out 'though the poet distils, the novelist tracks every branch and twig.'[6] Her tracking of 'every branch and twig' includes a variety of registers, texts, images and metaphorical devices from the most straightforward to the most complex.

One of the many registers in black speech is the Biblical:

We were expected to take part in the responses in church every Sunday in a far more positive way than most whites. The minister's function was to make you respond and participate. Jazz still has that feeling. Things shouldn't be over explained. There was awe and respect for the Bible.[3]

Not only do we hear images and rhythms from the Bible, but the grandmothers use its echoes. Here is the voice of Baby Suggs, calling black people to dance to her sermon of love in the woods: 'We flesh that weeps, laughs, dances ... Yonder they do not love your flesh.' (p 88) But even her love cannot outlast the destruction of her grandchildren, and 'Baby Suggs, holy, believed she had lied. There was no grace – imaginary or real.' (p 89) Thus Morrison extends the Biblical vocabulary to identify what will eventually break the heart of this unusually loving black ex-slave, who had brought a moment's grace into their suffering lives; 'the only grace they could have was the grace they could imagine.' (p 88) Interweaving such phrases indicates the way black people appreciated the music, the mystery, the complexity of one of few white discourses to which they were allowed access. Morrison acknowledges: 'They experienced joy in Biblical language and its cadences.'[9]

Morrison prefaces the novel with a quotation from Romans 9: 25: 'I will call them my people, which were not my people; and her beloved, which was not beloved.' Here Paul ponders, like Job, the evil and injustice on earth. Paul then goes on to state that the Gentiles, who had been outcast and despised, are now redefined as acceptable. Morrison skilfully suggests a context of hope, together with uncertainty about love. She uses a far better-known passage, from the Apocalypse, to represent the terror brought by the four men who recapture Sethe under the iniquitous Fugitive Slave Law; here the rhythms of crude white comment are interwoven with the Biblical image.

When the four horsemen came – schoolteacher, one nephew, one slave catcher and a sheriff – the house was so quiet they thought they were too late. Three of them dismounted, one stayed in the saddle, his rifle ready, his eyes trained away from the house to left and right, because likely as not the fugitive slave would make a dash for it. (p 148)

Black peoples' relationship to language was problematic because the use of African languages was restricted.

We were required to have another language, HIS language. Secondly we were not permitted to have a language within it. That is to say, Africanisms which survived in English were always called vulgar or slang (though some have been appropriated worldwide, like OK). In addition the combination of being a slave and being literate was supposed to be a contradiction in terms! So you came to language already manipulating it beautifully in terms of its metaphors, its similes, its power, its poetry. But we were always being told we were not articulate![9]

The Biblical allusions are skilful – Baby Suggs uses a present of blackberries to make pies which feed the whole community. Morrison makes myth specific, believable, with vivid detail: the ghost loves the burned bottom of bread. She uses language to make the everyday experiences of slaves alive to the reader; critics praise the lushness of her descriptions, but have not fully acknowledged Morrison's attention to the details of lives of hard physical work, such as Sethe pounding carbon to make ink. 'It was a book which required painstaking research, because there were almost no pictures (which usually start her writing). The tools, the everyday things – you had to use language in such a way that it had the effect of being concrete.'[1]

Conclusion

Morrison has transformed the ghost story to represent the curse of memory, a people haunted by its terrible past. She has created a family saga for a people who were denied families. She studies history in order to correct articulated prejudices, not with polemic which 'bores with its jargon' but with 'Homeric narrative strategies'[3] offering different points of view. We even sympathise with Sula, the whore who uses men, in the way we feel sorry for the blinded Cyclops, for an instant, in spite of his cruelty.

Her art gives us access to unfamiliar ways of seeing. For her as for her story-telling people there are no closed stories, always the possibility of telling it better, improvising in a fresh way like jazz – even giving the dead a voice. She can convey horror with occasional humour, from gentle to ironic. Morrison operates at the limits of language, voicing what had been concealed, telling the unthinkable without histrionics or anger. 'Anger cannot sustain you or last – it is only *art* which can translate this pain of slavery.'[6] Her art has achieved new prose for this terrifying topic.

Morrison's work is in the tradition of the great American novel, from Melville's *Moby Dick* to Bellow's *Herzog*, of rethinking structure and language, courageously tackling the vast themes of good and evil, sin and possible redemption. She has created a new structure, which incorporates elements of slave narrative, poetry, a prose poem of the dead, some stream-of-consciousness. *Beloved* includes not only folklore – the belief that the passions of the living keep ghosts alive – but elements of fairytale, as her outcast heroine survives against all odds. All the black characters 'have the essential *virtue* of fairytale heroes and exact our primitive affection unquestioningly. Toni Morrison's love for her people is Tolstoyan in its detail.'[14] And it is Tolstoyan in its respect for the beliefs, strength and potential of the poorest, the outcast. But Tolstoy's theories can lead to stasis, whereas Morrison points a way for her community to combat exploitation.

Possibly a new feminist poetics is needed to do justice to her range of discourses, her adaptation of black texts, speech and arts. Her techniques represent physical agony, reflection, murder, growth, dream and damnation. Her prose ambitiously interweaves fact and poetry. Her skilfully crafted structure opens and closes with the supernatural, within the context of real suffering: 'There is a loneliness that can be rocked. ... Then there is a loneliness that roams. It was not a story to pass on ....' (p 275)

Critics have praised the recent novel as a masterpiece, yet it has not been presented for a prize yet in America, perhaps a sign that black women writers still suffer marginalisation. A.S. Byatt considers 'Toni Morrison has always been an ambitious artist, sometimes almost clotted or tangled in her own brilliant and complex vision. *Beloved* has a new strength and simplicity. This novel gave me nightmares, yet I sat up late, paradoxically smiling to myself with intense pleasure at the exact beauty of the singing prose.'[14] The male critic Allan Massie states that Morrison is approaching greatness more surely than anyone else who has begun to publish in the United States in the last quarter of a century.[15]

Notes

1   Interview with R. Nadelson, *The Guardian*, 30 September 1987. All references to this interview are numbered 1.

2   *The Times,* 18 March 1988.
3   Interview with Paul Bailey, BBC Radio 3, 14 August 1982. All references to this interview are numbered 3.
4   M. Evans, ed, *Black Women Writers,* Pluto, 1985, p 343.
5   *Black Women Writers,* p 344.
6   Author's interview with Toni Morrison at the Institute of Contemporary Arts on 23 February 1988. All references to this interview are numbered 6.
7   *Black Women Writers,* p 171.
8   See article on *The Color Purple* in C. Kaplan, *Sea Changes,* Verso, 1986.
9   Interview with Christopher Bigsby on *Kaleidoscope,* BBC Radio 4, 23 february 1988. All references to this interview are numbered 9.
10   Margaret Atwood in *The New York Times* , 13 September 1987. All references to this review are numbered 10.
11   *Black Women Writers,* p 345.
12   B. Smith, 'Toward A Black Feminist Criticism' in *New Feminist Criticism,* ed E. Showalter, Virago, 1986.
13   When asked what Guitar symbolises, Morrison replied, 'Guitar represents an idea which was bothering me – most of my books start that way – what flying meant as a piece of history, and prophecy. I examine what education makes a black man feel comfortable, what their learning was, how to fly, take risks and dangers, what they learn of value from other men, starting with folklore. Milkman needs an older boy whose political logic becomes clear, as compared to the property-owning father. I push all the characters out as far as can be. In the end I have the friendship triumph again. Guitar can no longer fire at him so any fight has to be equal, fought with respect. In the end it does not matter which one dies in the killing arms of his brother.'
14   A. S. Byatt in *The Guardian,* 16 October 1987. All references to this article are numbered 14.
15   *The Times,* 18 March 1988.

7
Caribbean Women Writers

The writing of Caribbean women maps an exciting new territory of world literature. Many of the experiences chronicled cross national boundaries and are shared by women elsewhere. The lively examination of gender and race has produced a distinctive body of literature in the last decade.

It is not farfetched to perceive close parallels between the freeing of nations from the demeaning views of colonisers and the freeing of women from the degrading opinions of patriarchy. Women's experience of the power politics of gender have affinities with attitudes in the Caribbean towards the cultural imperialism of Britain, the United States and France. And the colonial inheritance of the English, French and Spanish languages is complicated by the multiple origins of the population resulting from slavery, conquest and settlement. Yet radical differences between the divergent parts of the Caribbean do not prevent a sharing of strong loyalties to cultural origins, together with a strong sense of marginality in relation to those three languages.

The Caribbean is composed of many distinct islands and two countries in Central America, Belize and Guyana. They are distant from each other not only geographically, but socially. The social and linguistic diversity partially reflects historical European rivalries and conquests. The islands of Guadeloupe and Martinique are an integral part of France, thus the superb novelist Simone Schwarz-Bart writes in French. Some islands feel too near the US for their cultural or economic good, and of course Spanish-speaking Cuba is experimenting with a radically different political and cultural regime.

Their structures and populations differ. Trinidad had a large component of indentured labourers from East India, who often identify with Hindu and Indian values – especially when the Indian cricket team arrives. Much land, as in Barbados, was given over to sugar plantations, money from which funded European capitalism. Many islands possess their own patois (which Jamaicans spell Patwah) or Creole, while Grenada and St Lucia developed a language which makes use of African, English and French words. Merle Collins writes: 'All the islands have their own language incorporating African, English and French words, because of the historical experience. The spelling is different as these have not been written languages. Perhaps Creole is the best word to designate them.'[1]

The cultural cross-fertilisation has produced new growth and new forms in many arts. This is well-known in music since calypso and reggae have gained international acclaim. The variety of rhythms and words reflect many African, Amerindian and European sources. Such variety is displayed in the creative work of women, such as cooking and textiles, and in religion. Many forms of Christianity, Islam and Hinduism and voodoo flourish, resulting in constant cross-fertilisation – and relatively little violence, if compared to Sri Lanka or Bangladesh.

Most Caribbeans experience a dual cultural identity, through the language they spoke with other children, and through the language insisted on in schools. This dual cultural identity endows the women novelists I examine with an *enlarged* social vision, which Toni Morrison proudly proclaims as a feature of black women writers today.

Many of these newly published writers have lived between two societies: the Caribbean and British. Their knowledge of two societies, and two differing attitudes to womanhood and personal relationships, undoubtedly enriches their work. The migrant community is well-travelled, bringing a spectrum of other life styles. Today these women have a wider range of options than their mothers, even though the successful, like Merle Collins and Joan Riley, still feel marginalised.

There are similarities between those still living in the Caribbean and their immigrant sisters: they all pay tribute to American women writers, as inspiration in their creative development. Black music has been one of the most important sources of linguistic and rhythmic innovation. Sounds recollected from childhood invade their prose and poetry. Black British speech rhythms have already been overlaid and extended by varied Caribbean, and occasionally African, word patterns. These suggest links between a range of black voices which go far beyond their immediate cultural experiences. Many have written exploratory pioneering work, in long short stories or fables from their own cultural story-telling traditions. They often examine the harsh realities of young motherhood, social humiliations or recurrent unemployment. They also bear

witness to the independence and creativity which have character-
ised black female life for centuries.

They have set themselves aims which recall Toni Morrison and
Alice Walker:

> We have been caricatured as ignorant drudges, as evil prostitutes,
> as castrators of men. We know otherwise. We embody a largeness
> and a continuity far beyond these limiting stereotypes. We are
> laying claim to selfhood, separate from and equal to men,
> demanding recognition not only from the host society but from
> our own community. We write in order to create new models for
> our young and a new fortitude. We are in search of our hidden
> triumphs that helped us to survive the horrors of the past,
> triumphs that have gone unheeded before.[2]

I have chosen four women each of whom represents a distinct
approach and culture: Merle Collins from Grenada, now living in
London, Grace Nichols from Guyana, Jean Rhys from Dominica and
Olive Senior from Jamaica. Despite significant variations, these
women share features which are both personal and socio-political.
They have suffered from the imbalance between men and women,
which leads them to explore problems of identity as well as
inequality.

In many of their novels those who survive form a close relationship with other women. Indeed the critics Merle Hodge, Merle
Collins and Hermione McKenzie indicate several similarities. The
preponderance of the matriarchal family derives from 'a synthesis
of an African cultural survival with the realities of slavery; women
live in societies where their emotional and sexual relationships have
been destroyed by humiliating economic conditions'.[3] They are
often left as single head of the household, and without a stable
income. This economically depressed condition makes the woman
as 'sexually vulnerable as she was in the darker days of her
history'.[4] Zee Edgell illustrates this in her novel *Beka Lamb* (1982);
when the heroine's friend Toycie becomes pregnant, she is rejected
by both boyfriend and educational system.

They approach writing with double anxiety, since their models
were either male authors or women nurturing children. In the overcoming of these obstacles, Caribbean novelists have created women
characters who are self-supporting, enduring. Significantly, the
stories about Caribbean women's passage into maturity are more
positive than the novels of Jean Rhys, which are about white or

Creole women. This positive approach is one they share with black American women novelists.

Black women writers also display a capacity for joy which breaks through the most dismal scenarios; a joy that is transmitted by grandmother or aunt if the mother is exhausted, or ill – or dead. In their own countries the women relatives always helped out, but in Britain the extended family is lost. Their newly revalued traditions and discourse face formidable enemies in the long hours worked by mothers and in television, threatening the very survival of their languages – unless they continue to write. The novel has a vital role today in examining Caribbean experience.

Olive Senior

I begin with Olive Senior, partly because she lives in Jamaica, one of the most populated of the ex-British-dominated islands, partly because she won the Commonwealth Writers Prize in 1988, but mainly as her writing displays features of the other women to be mentioned, and the two cultures, of 'standard' English and Caribbean speech.

She places herself in the second wave of Caribbean writers. The first wave comprised mainly men: V. S. Naipaul, Samuel Selvon, George Lamming, Mittelholzer etc. and two women, Louise Bennett and Jean Rhys. As in the US, it has taken a little longer for most women to find the confidence – and the time – to write. Many began, like Olive Senior, with poetry. Her first volume *Talking about Trees* was published by a small press in Kingston. It contains some powerful personal verse: 'Alone I will walk through the glass / and become.' (p 1) And awareness of history:

Listen child, said my father
from the quicksand of his life:
Study rivers. Learn everything.
Rivers may find beginnings
in the clefts of separate mountains
Yet all find their true homes
in the salt on one sea.

The volume which received the Commonwealth prize is *Summer Lightning* (1986). It is a collection of short stories, exploring the topics of childhood, pubescence, fathers never known, innocent children growing warily into a perplexing adult world, faith, what love might be, discipline, the irrelevance of education. Springville, where many take place, is not unlike the village in which Senior grew up. There, as a child, books seldom formed part of community consciousness. Senior comments:

> It's very difficult to be a writer in the Caribbean because you also have to hold down a job to earn a living, as I do. Our societies are not reading societies, so there is no public support for what you are doing, you're fairly isolated. People think you are crazy. One of the things that makes me pleased about winning this prize is that I'd like young people there to feel that writing is worth pursuing ... I grew up with little exposure to books. Of course we read English literature in High School. But before I went to school there was really no tradition of Caribbean writing. I come out of a largely oral tradition, where the Bible was the critical piece of literature. *Pilgrim's Progress* and uplifting moral tales were the only material around.[5]

Olive Senior grew up in a small community where story telling was important:

> because we had no other form of entertainment, not just as formal story telling in a sense that we were told stories at night – but that people in recounting their day to day activities were very dramatic, you know, developed a style of telling things very dramatically, and we children followed suit. We dramatised things, made them seem far more important than they really were.[6]

'Summer Lightning' the title piece of the collection, centres on a boy growing up, faced with a puzzling adult, a Rastafarian. He is just 'the old man' whom the boy does not understand, but gradually suspects of homosexual leanings. The narrative shows female ability to turn a possible limitation into a strength: Senior writes from one viewpoint, the boy's viewpoint, slowly suggesting the complex undercurrents created by adult needs. Her ending is brilliantly ambiguous:

> The boy jumped from the chair, for the old man, suddenly standing close to him was no longer looking coy or foolish. His hair was standing untidily from his head as always, his dirty merino collar rose above his shirt, he smelled the same way, but his

eyes were no longer weak and uncertain. They were firmly focused on the boy and they held a command. All through his body the boy suddenly felt drained and weak. Through a film like that covering the eye of his spirit level, he saw the man advance toward him.

Each story experiments with a different structure, a different register. 'Ballad' is written in Patwah to convey the narrowness of 'standard' English which the teacher had attempted to impose on the girl's writing, so removing its vitality. It opens unambiguously: 'Teacher ask me to write composition about The Most Unforgettable Character I ever Meet and I write three page about Miss Rilla and Teacher tear it up and say that Miss Rilla not fit person to write composition about and right away I feel so bad the same way I feel the day Miss Rilla go and die on me.' Like Jamaica Kinkaid in her brilliant short story 'Girl' Senior uses a monologue in order to foreground the impressions of a disregarded girl.

'Love Orange' also centres on a pubescent girl, in an apparently more straightforward narrative, but one enriched with poetic, unusual images about the difficulty of loving and expressing affection for the grandmother 'this tiny, delicate, slightly absurd old woman who lived for us only in the secret and mysterious prison of the aged' (p 13).

In her stories Senior represents women who are very important yet seem powerless. She considers

> this is the true state of the Caribbean woman in that she has, for the most part, responsibility for rearing and supporting children. She plays all the roles, disciplinarian, provider, nurturer. At the same time she is ambivalent in her dealings with men. She is powerful in the domestic sphere, but vulnerable in the realm of sexual relationships.[7]

Senior is understanding, like most black American writers, about the way black men have been unappreciated, and are becoming increasingly marginalised. She points out that there are many explanations: 'There are sociological reasons: some say that during slavery, when the women were owned by white men, black men had no role in terms of providing, or even caring. There are economic reasons, as the rate of unemployment is high and few men earn enough to support a family.'[8]

Another theme which Senior (and many of her contemporaries) examines is migration, above all emigration with the hope of self-betterment.

It's part of a Jamaican tradition. Jamaicans have emigrated in large numbers since the 1850s when they went to build the Panama railroad. In fact West Indians generally worked on most of the large construction projects in Latin America, including the building of the Panama Canal. Of course there was the large-scale migration to Britain in the 1950s. And there has been a tradition of going to the United States as well, since the nineteenth century. The whole notion of going abroad is perceived as a means by which you can improve your status in life. If you've been abroad you are automatically enhanced in the eyes of the people who stayed behind. Travel is important as a means of escape and as self-improvement.[9]

Hopes of travel and self-betterment, and the resulting disappointments are topics which recur in Caribbean writing. This is increasingly so since the 1950s with Paule Marshall writing about Barbadian immigrants in New York, and with the work of some of the younger women, such as Joan Riley who was sent from Jamaica to London at the tender age of ten. Hopes for travel, followed by bitter disillusion, are experienced by many of the lonely heroines created by Jean Rhys.

Jean Rhys

Jean Rhys, from Dominica, is the one white woman in this group, and significantly, the one whose name is best known. She adopted a genre made popular by women novelists in the eighteenth century – the romance. Rhys wrote for similar reasons to those of many forgotten women writers (see Dale Spender's study of them in *Mothers of the Novel*, 1987): to express feelings and to earn money. The romance may end happily in marriage, or tragically when the lover is lost. It can be read as an analysis of the female unconscious, the longings and fears which society represses, and politically, illustrating the ways in which a culture marginalises the 'second sex'. Romance creates a space for women.

Rhys came to England, alone, at the age of 26. She worked at lowly-paid jobs, in London and Paris, and wrote in her spare time, in her tiny rented room, pouring onto paper all the unhappiness she experienced. She often fell in love with the sort of men who would leave her miserable, and therefore chose a tragic ending for all her romances. Since the medieval romance, an important element of this genre has been the suggestion that fate, circumstances, are stronger than individuals. Such a tragic ending can be read as supporting the status quo, because the individual woman is powerless, caught up in beautiful, sad, uncontrollable emotions.

One of Jean Rhys' best known novels is *Wide Sargasso Sea* published in 1966. It is inspired by an episode in *Jane Eyre* when Rochester's first wife Bertha Mason burns down his house. This is an example of women's traditions helping each other, and of inter-textuality, of texts speaking to texts.

Bertha Mason represents both woman-as-victim and social fear of female sexuality. Rhys keeps closely to Charlotte Brontë's story to explore the dilemmas and unhappiness of 'creolised' women. This is a group whose confusion over identity and self-worth is seldom studied. Rhys attempts to explain the girl's descent into insanity by understanding her past. The story suggests that Bertha's madness – a favoured topic of many Victorian novels – is the result of personal rejection by the mother (who preferred her brother) and the result of living in a colonised environment. The rejected girl tries to cling to her Caribbean friend Tia, whose life she shares till they separate after a fight, separation causing her misery.

Rochester, the masterful male admired by Jane Eyre, made his fortune in the West Indies, running a slave plantation and marrying for money. Yet he is made to expiate his past before he is worthy of Jane. (In *Mansfield Park* also money made from exploitation of the then West Indies is at the root of the corruption of the upper middle class English.)

Rochester marries his first wife because he is the unentailed second son and must work for his living. He soon rejects her because her tastes were obnoxious to him. He describes her as 'dark' suggesting a mixture of race, and expresses shock at the islands' racial intermingling. 'Long, sad, dark alien eyes. Creole of *pure English descent* [my italics] she may be, but they are not English – or European either.' (p 67) Rochester typifies English prejudices; he is racist in making a dark woman into the scapegoat for his incapacity to love her fully or accept differences between peoples. He can thus justify his rejection of her.

Rejection leads to self-hatred, as in so many nineteenth-century women's novels, a self-rejection stressed through dream imagery. Towards the end of the novel, Rhys uses dream as Brontë had done, to convey unresolved dilemmas in the unconscious. Antionette tries to remember something 'she must do'. She dreams of the night when their house burned down, and imagines a reconciliation with

Tia: 'When I looked over the edge, Tia was there. She beckoned me and when I hesitated she laughed. I heard her say, You frightened?' (p 189). Thus the final suicide can read as not entirely tragic, but as reaffirmation of the relationship with Caribbean woman.

Exile, and subsequent marginalisation, are topics of many of Jean Rhys's widely read romances. Her lonely heroines find themselves exiled, like many other emigrants from the Caribbean, in a large metropolis where almost nobody accepts them. The women of her fiction resemble Jean Rhys in not finding any place in the literary Left Bank of Paris. She was an outsider among outsiders, living in streets smelling of poverty and hunger. The insightful novelist Elizabeth Bowen claimed: 'she showed an underworld of darkness and disorder where officialdom, the bourgeoisie and the police were the eternal enemies.' (*Drawn from Life*, p 166) Rhys can be said to represent the marginality of the woman exiled from her rural, island environment – unable to earn a decent living in an alien modern city.

Though Jean Rhys's women internalise their humiliations, they live out their suffering in the external world. I will analyse only one, fairly representative novel, out of the many set in Paris and London: *Good Morning Midnight* (1970). The heroine, Sasha, finds no decent room and is forced to live out her private suffering in public places. This novel recapitulates many familiar Rhys themes: the grey hopelessness of London life, the effects of poverty, longings for suicide. Sasha escapes to Paris, there made to realise how much the English are disliked, tolerated only when they have money. She overhears insults which alienate her mentally, while men humiliate her sexually.

Without realising it explicitly, Rhys articulates a feminist argument based on the economic, physical and psychological exploitation of women in a patriarchal, racist society. She depicts a culture which pays only lip service to the value of the individual, while exploiting the weak and economically dislocated. Her final pages recall those of Merle Hodge and Joan Riley in representing painful images of loneliness and emotional need. Through the fictional device of falling miserably in love, Rhys's dialectic of the self and the world is grounded in her experience of personal emotional disappointment, *and* as underpaid immigrant office worker.

More has been written about Jean Rhys than any other Caribbean woman. Francis Wyndham and Diana Melly have researched in the US and produced an interesting edition of her *Letters* (1984). H. Nebeker's *Critical Study*[10] is skilful. J. Moore comments: 'The women realise that their gender, poverty and powerlessness cause their vulnerability. In their societies, the impersonal and unequal power structures make both blackness and femaleness significant disadvantages'.[11] Rhys has been criticised for the 'passiveness' of her characters. Yet her novels can be read as quietly defiant in depicting women unable to fit the submissive roles assigned to them by colonialism. Merle Collins, the next writer to be discussed, foregrounds such issues explicitly.

Merle Collins

Merle Collins typifies the more politicised younger Caribbean writers now living in Britain. Proudly employing Creole in her prose and poetry, she is gaining an increasing audience for her readings, her talks, her criticism and above all, her writing.

In Grenada she enjoyed writing at school, and a women's collective helped with a dramatised presentation of one of her poems. Collins considers that this opportunity for discussion with friends is the most important help a writer can receive, as vital as 'a room of one's own'. Caribbean oral tradition provides criticism, and revaluation: 'Much of the early work in Grenada was presented orally to a responsive and supportive audience.'[12] She did not feel the need to publish until after the US invasion of Grenada in 1983, which put an end to their meetings as 'subversive'. She came to Britain where she was published by a black press. 'Black presses are as important to the black community as women's presses have been to women seeking expression.'

Her novel *Angel* (1987) was prompted by the desire, after the invasion of 1983, to understand what had happened to her community, in a historical sense. The political situation is not described as she wanted to 'get behind the headlines'. She discovered that there was little information on Grenada before the invasion 'as if it were a country of whose existence the British media seemed unaware'. The internal divisions 'which apparently led to some murders, including that of Maurice Bishop' take second place compared to the reactions of her people. She foregrounds the effects of language on self-image, and makes Grenadian as important as 'standard' English. As with James Joyce, it can be hard work to enter into the meanings of some of the vernacular phrases, though by the end of *Ulysses* we have been taught a new language, with force and beauty coming from the use of previously undervalued Gaelic.

The revaluing of the indigenous was among her intentions:

> In writing you can discuss the whole issue of the role of art, issues
> of language. To me it is vital that my writing makes a difference
> in the way people view themselves, interpret their history and see
> their self-image. It is important for us to use *both* languages, no
> longer feel one's own is worthless. It is essential to write for our
> community, to have these discussions within our community.[13]

Many different members of the community discuss contemporary
events in *Angel*. One woman recounts to a newly returned relation:

> Then after you work you piece o ground, put all your labour in it,
> when the cocoa they ask you to plant in between in its growth
> now, they takin away the piece of land from you and give you a
> new piece to do the same .... (p 10)

Collins' innovation is not to keep Grenadian for dialogue alone
but to weave it into direct free style, shifting into the characters'
thoughts:

> Then there was a loud crackling sound from the fire. Lord, ah is
> come back to this Grenada at a bad time. If only they didn lay off
> Allan at least we coulda put aside a little more money for bad times
> ahead. Ma Ettie clasped her hands and bowed her head. 'Lord, take
> a thought for the little children in that burning house.' (p 5)

Interestingly, when the Bible is quoted, the words are close to the
King James version. As Buchi Emecheta commented (see next
chapter) the words of the Bible are a shared formative influence on
many black writers, from James Baldwin in the US to the South
African writer Bessie Head.

Such switching between various discourses, in this brief extract,
implicitly underlines the richness of the cultural cross-fertilisation.
And Collins uses the women's own discourse to comment explicitly
on the political situation. So, in a letter, Angel's mother writes:

> Over here things not too bad but is real confusion in the land. You
> should see you boy Leader in form. To tell you the truth, Ezra, the
> country need a shake up like this, even tho I know the sort of
> person leader is. I not too sure I like the way they doing things.
> There is a lot of violence that startin up. I even hear that people

get kill, but everybody stout stout behind Leader. People thinkin
he is saviour. (p 6)

Her immigrant's perspective widens the study, which is further
enlarged by typographical innovation – the interspersing of
sentences in large black type. These are either political wall slogans,
or women's sayings, in fact sayings which are part of the communal
language, made into banner headlines: 'WE HA TO HOL ONE
ANOTHER UP. NUTTING DOESN HAPPEN BEFORE IT TIME.'
Like Dos Passos, Collins brings in the world of newspaper headlines; her invention is to include many statements from Grenadian
dialogue. She represents political issues through women's experience, like Grace Nichols.

Grace Nichols

Grace Nichols also emigrated to Britain (in 1977), but she grew up in
the very different context of Guyana, Central America. She has
published stories for children but is best known for *Whole of a Morning
Sky*, an autobiographical novel, and a cycle of poems *i is a long
memoried woman*, which won the Commonwealth Poetry Prize in 1982.

This attempts the same ambitious project as Toni Morrison in
Beloved: to trace the history of slavery. She goes back further, to
Africa, now only a memory of what has been lost, ending with the
Haitian revolution and the recognition 'I have crossed an ocean /I
have lost my tongue /from the roots of the old /one / a new one
has sprung'.

Whole of a Morning Sky (1987) sketches the political situation of the
1960s, while foregrounding its effects on her community. Grace
Nichols lives in her characters, using Creole to express their
thoughts and emotions. She is thus reclaiming her language heritage:

It's an act of spiritual survival on our part. It's a language our
foremothers and forefathers struggled to create and we're saying
that it's a valid, vibrant language ... I find it genuinely exciting.
Some Creole expressions are so vivid and concise, they have no
equivalent in English ... Difference, diversity, unpredictability
make me tick.[14]

Grace Nichols is interested in mythology, and the way it creates
archetypes which can prove destructive. Like Alice Walker she

rejects the image of the all-powerful white male God, together with biblical association of white, light and goodness, black with darkness and evil. 'We have got to come up with new myths and other images. White people have to be aware that what the white imagination has done is transfer their terror of darkness to a whole race.'[15]

In *i is a long memoried woman* the protagonist is a mythic figure, rejecting the slave stereotype of the dumb victim. A complex woman who speaks of her circumstances with vision, she becomes a priestess, who can employ sorcery when necessary. Her spirit wanders, she is allowed to meet women from other cultures 'up past the Inca ruins ... to God de Mudda'. This new pride in the past of black women is linked to a pride in Caribbean culture – 'one of the richest, most fascinating you can hope to find ... O.K. it has its poverty and backwardness but influences and mixtures – Amerindian, African, Asian, European ... worlds constantly interacting.'[16]

Conclusion

Merle Collins considers that writing is implicitly political today:

> It's an artificial debate whether one should be committed or not, because it's impossible to write what is not related to what people are actually experiencing. If you talk about flowers, the images will relate to the struggles happening around us. Caribbean women's writing echoes the experiences of a 'developing region' and the effects of colonisation.[17]

Colonisation and the recent emergence from it can be compared to women's gendered perception of themselves. Since the 1970s the Women's Movement has challenged traditions which excluded them from power. Women's fiction suggests useful models in the search for national identity in its revisioning of language and culture. These novels do not represent nationalist or feminist theory, but in their openendedness, their multiplicity, their sharing, they offer ways forward.

To read Caribbean women's fiction of the 1980s is to become aware of how a cultural map exceeds geographical limits. National boundaries have been extended imaginatively to accommodate recognition of the multicultural inheritance of the Caribbean and its internationalism.

Notes

1   Author's correspondence with Merle Collins, 3 August 1988.
2   L. Ngcobo, *Let It Be Told*, Pluto, 1987, pp 1–2.
3   H. McKenzie, 'Introduction: Caribbean Women Yesterday, Today and Tomorrow' in *The Caribbean Woman*, ed E. Braithwaite, special issue of *Savacou*, 13 July 1977, pp viii–xiv.
4   L. Mathurin, 'Reluctant Matriarchs' in *Savacou*, 13 July 1977, pp 1–6.
5   Interview on *Bookshelf*, BBC Radio 4, February 1988.
6   From a discussion with Joan Griffiths, recorded on 9 March 1987.
7   Discussion with J. Griffiths cited above.
8   Discussion with J. Griffiths.
9   Interview on *Bookshelf*, BBC Radio 4, February 1988.
10 H. Nebeker, *Jean Rhys: Woman in Passage*, Montreal: Eden Press, 1981.
11 J. Moore, 'Sanity and Strength in Jean Rhys's West Indian Heroines', in *Rocky Mountain Review of Language and Literature*, 41, 1987, pp 21–31. See also Laura Neisen de Abruna, 'Mother-Daughter Bonding in Caribbean Women's Writing', a paper given at the Institute of Commonwealth Studies on 23 May 1988. Ms. Abruna works at Ithaca College, Ithaca, New York.
12 This and the following quotations are from author's correspondence with Merle Collins, 3 August 1988.
13 This and quotations in the previous paragraph are from a talk given at the Institute of Contemporary Arts, 23 February 1988.
14 *Let It Be Told*, p 98.
15 *Let It Be Told*, p 101.
16 *Let It Be Told*, p 97.
17 Talk given at the ICA, 23 February 1988.

For more information on the Caribbean: Ken Campbell, *The Caribbean*, Macdonald, 1980; Douglas Taylor, *Languages of the West Indies*, Johns Hopkins Press, 1977, surveys Amerindian and creole languages; Roger D. Abrahams, *The Man-of-words in the West Indies*, Johns Hopkins, 1983, studies the expressive life of traditional villages.

8
Buchi Emecheta and Black Immigrant Experience in Britain

Buchi Emecheta has been selected to represent the views of black women immigrants to England. Over two million people have immigrated from the Third World to Britain, yet few have written about this experience, and even fewer women. Too often they have physically exhausting jobs, with low pay and little status. Emecheta considers that as black mothers work long hours in hospitals, kitchens, and offices, they are too tired to tell their children stories. Thus the writing of stories has a new cultural value.

Emecheta believes, like Toni Morrison, that fiction has a vital social responsibility now that the oral tradition is less strong. Fiction keeps racial memories alive – and helps to make sense of the community threatened by alien groups and values. Black American writers are fortunate in that English is their first language, unlike Emecheta, and they can draw, without translation, on the rich verbal discourse of their fellows. Emecheta, without women friends to share with, turned in her loneliness to the recording of her immigrant experience. Significantly she began with journalism; journalism highlights the uniqueness of the particular, helpful for a budding writer. Emecheta's first articles deal with poverty in London and the difficulties of adjusting to a different culture. For example, on assistance, she suffered doubly: the dole was degrading because Ibos consider it arrogant to give charity and degrading to receive it.

Emecheta is an Ibo, from Nigeria, and her novels reflect aspects of Ibo culture rather than wider African story-telling. She studied sociology part-time and is more interested in bearing witness than in creating rich discourse.

Buchi Emecheta is the focus of this chapter because she has produced eight well-reviewed books and described vividly the experiences of immigrant women. She represents those with a distinct mother tongue, from a different culture, but using English for their writing.

113

The adjective 'black' is often used to describe Asian Indian communities. However, their cultures are so distinct that they deserve to be differentiated, particularly when discussing their writing. The Anglo-Asian community in Britain is large and growing, and demands a whole book to do it justice. It can boast writers of the stature of Anita Desai and Suniti Namjoshi. Desai's work ranges from foreign views of her community to incisive studies of contemporary India, with portraits of men as compelling as those of her female characters. She displays a growing maturity of vision with *In Custody* (published in 1987 and a runner-up for the Booker Prize) and *Baumgarten's Bombay* (1988), the story of a man without a country. Namjoshi exploits Indian fables, transforming them with her punchy feminist messages: '"And what do you want?" Lord Vishnu said to the girl. "I want human status." "Ah, that is much more difficult," and the god hedged and appointed a commission.'[1]

Cultural differences make it difficult to respond knowledgeably to Afro-Caribbean and Asian writers; a second book will look at Asia. Yet they face a common oppression and many believe the way ahead is to fight collectively. An Asian collective has now published its prose and poetry in *Right of Way* (1988), a skilful selection of short pieces on India and England in many stimulatingly differing registers and discourses.[2]

Asian and Afro-Caribbean women are fighting for women's rights, but hesitate to use the word 'feminist', feeling it somewhat sullied by exclusiveness, even racism. This has produced interesting debates on the links between women's consciousness-raising and politics. Increasing account is taken of the way in which class has distorted perceptions. And all Asian and Afro-Caribbean writers share the aim to create positive, varied images of their women, combatting together the negative cultural myths about immigrants.

My approach to Buchi Emecheta will be to explore her ideas, through her own words, her works, and through comparisons with other writers. She began writing for herself, as outsider and mother. To her surprise she discovered, like many women novelists since the 1960s, that her intimate story would interest many readers. Later the implicit critique of society, through her particular experiences, became more explicit, politicised. (The favourite term now is 'political', in that analyses of women's exploitation in the home and workplace stress a social dimension which must be addressed through politics if it is to be redressed.) Emecheta reveals growing awareness of issues of racism, multiculturalism, and exploitation of media images, paralleled in the declarations of American women writers. Her own words (in a generously long interview given me), convey some of the similarities and differences. And in order not to study her in a void, I mention two outstanding African novelists. Her cultural priorities and views on the treatment of the marginalised will emerge through her statements, a suitable vehicle for someone from a rich oral tradition. This is followed by a chronological overview of her novels.

Emecheta is one of the most prolific novelists of the black immigrant community in Britain. Yet English is her third language; she spoke Ibo with her parents and Yoruba at school. In order to get published, to have a readership, she must use English 'which will never be my emotional language'.* This typifies the alienation of many African immigrants: alienation from their country, their culture, their people, their sustaining community, and – appalling for a writer – from the very discourse in which they naturally express their reactions and feelings.

Emecheta married at sixteen and immediately produced babies. Her husband soon sailed to England, hoping for higher pay after studying here. She persuaded her in-laws to let her join him as she had a librarian's qualification, a passport to a steady job. She joined him at the age of nineteen, with two small children. Her response to the greyness, poverty and racism which they (and so many immigrants) have undergone is vividly depicted in *Second-Class Citizen* (1974). This autobiographical novel reveals the day-to-day problems and restrictions heaped on immigrant mothers attempting to improve their own lives and those of their children.

Alice Walker considers that Emecheta 'integrates the profession of writer into the cultural concept of mother/worker she retains from Ibo society. Just as the African mother had traditionally planted crops and pounded maize ... with her baby strapped on her back ...'[3] Emecheta is a writer and a mother because she is *both*. She manages a cultural perspective that precludes self-pity, as her ambition is also for the five children to whom the book is dedicated. Walker concludes:

Though *Second-Class Citizen* is not stylistically exciting ... it is no less valid as a novel. And a good one. It raises fundamental questions about how creative and prosaic life is to be lived and to what purpose, which is more than some books, written while

* denotes author's interview with Buchi Emecheta, 14 June 1988.

one's children are banished from one's life, do. And *Second Class Citizen* is one of the most informative books about contemporary African life that I have read.'[4]

The question of how the creative and prosaic life is to be lived by women is raised in many other black women's writings, from Paule Marshall's 'From the Poets in the Kitchen' (1983) to Barbara Burford's *The Threshing Floor* (1986). Emecheta shares this preoccupation, implicit in her early work, but overt now after a decade of consciousness-raising from sisters, most notably Alice Walker in *In Search of our Mothers' Gardens* (1983), emphasising the creativity of the black mother/worker.

Emecheta continues to work hard, as mother and writer simultaneously. Her five children still live at home, though she is planning to buy them flats. She started a publishing firm, Ogwugwu Afor, with her journalist son, to provide a needed platform and financial backing to black artists. Added to these commitments, she feels the need to help her extended family in Nigeria 'where I support thirty-one people!'.[5] The extended family can prove onerous as well as caring. Yet she praises its help, so lacking to English mothers, because her mother-in-law aided her all day while she worked, and even shared feeding.

Emecheta therefore considers, like American novelists, that the image of the black woman deserves revaluation:

> Women in old Africa were not all that free, but they had strong relevance in their societies. Housework was never regarded as a minor job, because in a society where to get fuel and prepare the meal takes all day, it is a crucial job ... The Black woman learnt to survive, and adapted so that in the Ibo area of Nigeria, she could even organise and fight her own wars. One example is the so-called 'Aba riots' of the late 1920s, led by women. Interestingly, those women were praised by their husbands, so much so that they became legendary figures, and we still sing their heroic deeds.[6]

Imparting a heroic stature to their foremothers is what Paule Marshall and Alice Walker are also achieving, through their praise-song and studies of hitherto neglected black writers of the past. All prove that the black woman is remarkably creative and enterprising even while her labour is exploited by society and her self-worth culturally pilloried.

'Black women all over the world should re-unite and re-examine the way history has portrayed us.'* That battlecry from Emecheta might have been uttered by many another, from Maya Angelou to the South African writer Bessie Head. However such similarities should not make one forget that Emecheta's cultural background differs from that of writers from the American South, and of those women who have stayed in Africa.

Emecheta's Cultural Experiences

'English is my third language,' she observes. 'It sounds colourless and grey because of translation. Ibo uses colourful phrases, many-syllabled words, less simplistic story-telling.'* Thus Emecheta cannot incorporate all the richness of her mother tongue into her novels, whereas Toni Morrison and Alice Walker, when fore-grounding the actual dialogue of their women, not only enrich written discourse, but also make a political statement about the value of their culture.

Emecheta is alienated from her mother tongue by colonialism, and cut off from many other Ibo women by Britain's class-ridden society. Since the majority of immigrants are forced to take menial jobs, such as cleaning, they can feel too embarrassed to be easy with her, 'whereas in Africa there is so little water that there is more equality among women: "I'll look after your child while you fetch water." '*

Such sharing has not disappeared from the American South, nor has the story-telling of older women in the extended family. Emecheta praises the stories of 'grandmothers and aunts who brought me up' but observes sadly that story-telling is dying in immigrant groups 'because mothers work such long hours and have to leave their children alone, as I did, with no female relatives near'.* Thus the rich Afro-American traditions of fable, animal imagery, oracy (as opposed to literacy), moralities, spoken tales, are dying out in Britain. Such loss differentiates Emecheta from her American sisters. She is less experimental in discourse and structure, less inventive in form, more cut off from the varied traditions of her people. She tries to recapture these by returning to Africa in the summer.

The dream of African immigrants is to go home, and stay there. The weather is so much better in Lagos, it helps you to relax. But you can only afford to do that if you find a well-paid job. I manage the summer there, so I keep my two worlds, my two cultures.*

Emecheta's early cultural experiences in Nigeria were of a colonised country: 'We all sang Rule Britannia at school and looked on England as our mother country.'* At that time the American South was struggling to implement anti-racist legislation. The Civil Rights movement gave American black people a profile and a pride which has not been equalled for black people in Britain.

Nigeria under English rule imposed both the English educational system and sectarian Protestant religion. Schools, as in the Caribbean, taught only 'standard' English to prepare for English examinations, with no respect for, or even mention of, the cultures in which they were living. Christian churches inculcated the worship of a god depicted as white; nevertheless they became central institutions in many American Southern and African communities. And they were the focus, the springboard, for social work (Alice Walker needed to collaborate with her church when working with young girls) while being the main outlet for singing, ritual and religious imagery. We hear Biblical language in all their writings – though in Emecheta the rhythms have not entered so forcefully, despite her allusions to parables.

Emecheta recognises that the Methodist church her family attended was rigid yet does not consider it paradoxical to adhere to much of its moral teaching. Some of its tenets such as 'finish whatever you thought fit to begin' aid her writing. Her mind is not colonised. She accepts Methodist rulings on sex and will not allow her children to disobey them; but she has translated Christian faith into a form compatible with an African outlook:

Heaven is down here, on earth. When somebody dies they go back into the earth. The land was here before we came, we are all just passing through ... I try to go to church every Sunday, and praying I equate with the African way of talking to oneself. A mother will say 'God, make my child be in a good temper today'. It's making prayer work, God's spirit inside you.*

This African spirituality resembles Shug's in *The Color Purple* – though Emecheta has not yet transmuted it into her fiction, except in a few parts of *The Rape of Shavi*.

After the hard labour of bringing up five small children on her own, while working and studying sociology at The London School of Economics, Emecheta now has a little time at last to read. Her education in Africa had been so traditionally English that it was only in London that she began the stimulating discovery of black writers. She particularly enjoys Maya Angelou, Zora Neale Hurston, Toni Morrison and Toni Cade Bambara. 'I love the way they use their colloquial language, it's meant to be read aloud, it's so musical. And there's a younger woman, who I taught in Creative Writing classes, Gloria Naylor – she uses lively, experimental English.'*

Time for reading and teaching on an MA course has crystallised Emecheta's perceived cultural priorities. At school she had accepted the idea of the Devil as black; now the freeing of language for all blacks, and the improving of the images used for women, are her articulated aims, not just embedded in the day-to-day account of an immigrant mother with an increasingly frustrated and violent husband. In recent writing she includes more discourses than her own, particularly that of Jamaicans: 'I have tried to incorporate Jamaican rhythms, such as "God dies for the truth" while writing about the dilemmas of blacks born in Britain. At last I have the courage to say "I write for blacks." '*

Autobiographical Writing

Emecheta continues to incorporate autobiography as an integral part of her fiction. *Head Above Water* (1986), her autobiography, follows the tribulations of *Second-Class Citizen* with an account of how she successfully emerged from condemned housing to a digni-fied, fulfilling life. It offers a constructive image of a black immigrant mother refusing to accept the few denigrating categories first thrust on her. *Head Above Water* depicts a slow improvement, not in her own situation alone: 'There are more blacks going to university, more Afro-Caribbean studies, more books by black writers studied in schools – though seldom on show in bookshops or libraries and the media. I still consider myself marginalised. In my present book I deal with the many problems and prejudices which exist for immigrants in Britain *now*.'*

In Emecheta are resemblances to many other women, especially working class women with large families, or single parents. They were categorised as 'problem' by the social services, and society. When I studied her books with an adult class we agreed that her experiences reflected those of many white as well as black women.

Maya Angelou also makes autobiography the mainspring of her

fiction, and claims that, though she uses the first person singular, she is talking about the third person plural – what it's like to be a human being. Unlike Angelou, Emecheta does not write poetry. However her prose could be said to demonstrate some of the polemical fervour of the South African writer Bessie Head. Both care about the values of old Africa and underline qualities which have been virtually unnoticed by whites. Both work for their communities and speak out for them.

Parallels With Bessie Head

Emecheta and Bessie Head have never met yet they share many perceptions about Africa. Both were born there yet not allowed to study their indigenous cultures. School imposed a wholly British syllabus. This has not been a complete disadvantage in novel-writing, because the African approach to story-telling is so different that their reading of English nineteenth-century novels has given them two rich, varied traditions to draw on. It has also forced them to write in a language which has become virtually an international esperanto. They can be read worldwide and appreciated by many distant women, thus creating new traditions of women's writing.

Both are exiles from the countries of their birth, South Africa and Nigeria. Head's experiences were so ghastly that she fled to Botswana; Emecheta came to London after her husband. They use their knowledge of two cultures to enrich their work and widen their study of their societies. These comparisons of differing cultural behaviour and attitude demonstrate that fiction, as Angela Carter claims, is often truer than fact.

Emecheta and Head reach out through personal problems to community issues. If one maintains that writers' fictionalising of an argument is partly guided by their social and artistic traditions one might trace the influence of recent history and its stories in their approach. Their childhood experiences of injustice (Emecheta was orphaned young) and life in racist societies in formative adolescent years have affected their structures. In addition to these shaping experiences are their impressions and meditations on living in exile - and elements they have *chosen* from their history and its stories. The story-telling of their people has stimulated them to add elements of fable and oral discourse. Furthermore, they have adapted the European novelistic tradition, which often makes falling in love central, to include opposing cultural attitudes to relationships. They skilfully exploit this uneasy link to suggest freer futures, where men and women can live more honestly together.

Bessie Head's work for co-operatives and Emecheta's printing firm help in training blacks, giving them pride in their creative abilities, allowing them outlets in areas generally dominated by white patriarchal firms. Her printing firm provides a much needed forum for black writers, as she knows:

> Until my company started, the covers of African novelists all bore drawings or photographs of Africans, so relegating them to the 'African' section of bookshops and libraries, where they were seldom read. When I began to search for a publisher I was told I must think of a mythical 'average' reader; as he would find my name unpronounceable, I must change it. One American publisher even suggested changing my nose!
>
> I set my early books in Africa, but the intelligentsia was not ready for that. The English prefer Jackie Collins, writing about dreams and fantasies. In *The Rape of Shavi* I attempted fantasy, but the ending turned out to be tragic … My stories are too real, and I am marginalised as Black and a woman. But I have this urge to go on writing. TO WRITE IS TO BE COMMITTED.*

Her sense of commitment is widening, as is her use of writing: children's stories, aimed frequently at black children, essays, articles – and a disquisition on the near future in *The Rape of Shavi* (1983). Here, as in Marge Piercy's searing novel *Woman on the Edge of Time* (1979), destructive technology is repudiated in favour of a subsistence economy – where women are treated with greater equality, since everyone must work hard together.

Emecheta is critical of some aspects of feminism as she considers that white women are too proud, too unsupportive, locked in images imposed on them by men (though many feminists would claim they are fighting these male-imposed images). 'The white girl pupil is encouraged to play the delicate, beautiful lady, an attitude that survives from slave society. But matters are far worse for the black girl because her myth is that of the mammy, fat, a headscarf to cover her ugly, crinkly hair.'[7] White feminist notions should not be transported without studying the situation in Africa: 'Polygamy can even help a young wife, by giving her the freedom to study. We are not quite ready for White Women's Liberation.'[8] Like Alice Walker who distances herself as 'womanist', neither shrinks from describing the ill-treatment meted out by some males to women in their community.

Emecheta and Chinua Achebe

There are over two million black immigrants in Britain, yet few have been encouraged to write about their experiences. Women have found it almost impossible until recently, because many of them work such long hours in offices, hospitals, sweatshops and homes. It is significant to compare their situation with male writers, and I have selected Chinua Achebe, to highlight some of the differences.

Chinua Achebe was more fortunate than Emecheta, because he came to London to study full-time, after completing a degree in Nigeria. The title of his first novel *Things Fall Apart* (1958) is a quotation from Yeats, evidence of the greater opportunity to read and study granted to the African male. He took full advantage of this and developed concise, skilful forms, more polished than the structures of the overworked Emecheta.

He contrasts Western civilisation unfavourably to African, a subject Emecheta is embarked on now (in articles and in *The Rape of Shavi*). His novel (part of a trilogy) centres on the tragedy of a brave tribal leader confronting the first white missionaries. The hero is finally forced to suicide, to escape the results of his rash courageous stand against the white colonials. The macabre is handled with telling restraint, the emotion with irony:

> Obierika, who had been gazing steadily at his friend's dangling body, turned suddenly to the District Commissioner and said furiously: 'That man was one of the greatest in Umuofia. You drove him to kill himself; and now he will be buried like a dog.' The Commissioner went away, taking three or four of the soldiers with him. In the many years in which he had toiled to bring civilisation to different parts of Africa he had learnt a number of things. One of them was that a D.C. must never attend to such undignified details as cutting down a hanged man from a tree .... (*Things Fall Apart*, p 147)

Achebe and Emecheta bring Ibo qualities into English. Both display vividness, economy, directness, a sense of the rape of their culture. The vitality of many non-English languages, like theirs, is now enlarging English. The novel is being continually extended by other traditions of story-telling, and by cultural perspectives which break out of national confines and make it international.

Emecheta's Novels

Second-Class Citizen

Emecheta's aims were not international at first, but personal, to recount *her* story. However this individual woman has captivated readers as she represents the outsider who comes to England only to find that the streets are not paved with the proverbial gold. Proud, ambitious and determined to maintain her independence, she battles on; despite a violent husband and poverty, she manages to bring up five children without losing sight of her dreams.

Emecheta gives insights into the psychological processes under racism:

> She who only a few weeks previously would have accepted nothing but the best had by now been conditioned to expect inferior things, so did not waste her time looking for a room in a clean, desirable neighbourhood. Whenever she went into big clothes stores, she would automatically go to the counters carrying soiled and discarded items, afraid of what the shop assistants might say. Even if she had enough money for the best, she would start looking at the sub-standard ones and then work her way up. This was where she differed from Francis [her husband] and the others. They believed that one had to start with the inferior and stay there; being black meant being inferior. (*Second-Class Citizen*, p 60)

Thrown out by Nigerian landlords averse to children, Emecheta's protagonist-self Adah made the devastating discovery that most adverts for rooms stated 'Sorry, no coloureds'. So 'Adah learned to pinch her nose when talking over the phone, in order not to sound African' (p 68). Even so, she was refused everywhere, and was near despair until she finally found two rooms in the house of an aged Nigerian, who could not let his rooms easily since two white women had died in them. Through her analysis of him, Emecheta offers insights into the Nigerian 'ghetto':

> There was another group of Nigerians who came to England in the late forties, when still a colony. They were well-educated in secondary schools, and had to come to England to get a Law degree to be eligible for poshy vacant jobs under forthcoming self-rule. However most of those who sought the kingdom of the eligibles, like the seeds of that sower in the Bible, fell on the wayside to be trodden upon by passersby. (p 68)

Second-Class Citizen centres on Emecheta's unquestioning acceptance that caring for her children is the essential part of her life, even while working full-time and studying to improve her prospects. Caring motherhood, with all its anxieties, was emphasised in Britain by the women novelists of the 1960s, such as Margaret Drabble in *The Millstone* (1965), where she depicts love for a child as her heroine's most important relationship. The sudden appearance of white novels dealing with women's intimate lives in the sixties, and of black women's novels after 1970, suggests a *zeitgeist*, a spirit of the age: groups of women recording their experiences as mothers and artists, simultaneously, without obvious influence from each other, but while cultural attitudes were changing towards women. I would argue that their novels speeded the transformation of societal attitudes.

Obviously when women write from their own intimate experience their fiction will draw heavily on lived reality. Indeed feminism has opened up the structuralist view that writing deals with a language world, by allowing the study of the lives of women writers. Feminist literary critics realise that female frustrations, restrictions, fears and loves colour their work. Thus women novelists should not feel the need to apologise if their fictionalising is autobiographical. Certainly, Emecheta's *Second-Class Citizen* is an autobiographical account of her life: from orphaned childhood to success in school, followed by an unhappy marriage, five pregnancies and a cold existence in a London tenement. She combines the attraction of story-telling with insight into the difficulties of immigrant life. Emecheta admires the story-telling of the African women who brought her up and used stories to teach morals. This dual purpose, to entertain and instruct, shows an interesting link between African and Renaissance aims in literature: to delight and instruct.

> I wanted to tell a good story as I enjoy reading, and just put in a few ideas to make people think. I believe in learning without tears. Every good novel should depict the idea of the author and the society in which they live.[9]

Emecheta's story-telling is direct and compelling. As a child she longed to go to school, but the family money was spent on educating her brother. One day she felt so desperate that she marched into school with a stolen slate. When she returned home there was a big hullabaloo going on. Pa had been called from work, Ma was with the police being charged with child neglect, and the child that had caused all the fuss was little Adah, staring at them all, afraid, yet triumphant ... So that was how Adah started school. (p 12)

The simple language grips the reader in the old-fashioned pleasure of a good read. However on close analysis this realist text proves more subtle, including the three modes described by the structuralist Benveniste.[10] Emecheta frequently uses the *declarative* mode, as in the paragraph above, to declare a state of affairs to the reader. She often includes *imperative* sentences imparting 'knowledge' to the reader; statements with elements of propaganda, instructing the reader to observe conflict:

Every door seemed barred against them, nobody would consider accommodating them, even when they were willing to pay double the normal rent. (p 77)

And she is fond of the *interrogative* which invites the reader to produce answers to questions explicitly (or implicitly) raised: 'Why didn't the authorities permit the mothers of young babies to stay with their sick offspring in hospital?' (p 68). This is unsubtle compared to Brecht, but both alternately take us in and distance us as they question the ideology of society. The interrogative mode is useful for dealing with collisions and contrasts between what white liberals think and what actually happens.

Emecheta writes as she speaks; this can prove a drawback, since she includes slovenly expressions and unnecessary repetitions. She imparts a restful, though occasionally annoying, sense of chatting to you. Yet *Second-Class Citizen* is one of the most borrowed books from London libraries. Why? She satisfies a need, like good journalism, to enquire into other people's lives. It is significant that her first book *In The Ditch* (1972) was first printed in short parts in the *New Statesman* magazine. Like a journalist she is preoccupied with the uniqueness of the particular. She enjoys reportage, and like many male novelists exploits reportage to reinvigorate fiction. She has committed herself to the historical mode rather than fabulation.[11] She interprets the historical forces that have moulded women like herself. She views the setbacks as social (like a Marxist) and capable of improvement; not as the ineradicable evil posited by many twentieth-century writers, such as Anthony Burgess.

Part of her conviction stems from the capacity to depict social predicaments, in England and Nigeria. She understands the way blacks can hurt each other in their ghettos: 'The real discrimination came more from our own countrymen giving [each other] inferiority feelings.' (p 76) She gives insights into her own Ibo culture: 'In Lagos you had to learn to control your temper, which Adah was taught was against the law of nature.' (p 8)

These comments are integrated into the main story, which carries the reader along with jounalistic style. Like Edna O'Brien and Margaret Drabble, Emecheta has turned her unhappy experiences to financial advantage to support herself and her family. And she proves Drabble's dictum that women today are fortunate in having causes to write about.

Emecheta incorporates these causes into her novels, like the mid-Victorians whom she read at school. She shows the middle-class what their society does to someone considered inferior. The parallels with Charlotte Brontë's *Jane Eyre* (1847) are instructive: both heroines are poor, unloved outsiders; both relish their unimaginative education as it is a means to independence. They are aided by a self-image that enables them to withstand humiliations and economic hardships. In the end by insisting that the 'inferior' have emotional needs and rights, they gain love: Jane Eyre allegorically, after the blinding of Rochester and her improbable inheriting of a fortune. Emecheta finds men wanting, but gains consolation in intense devotion and caring for her children.

Emecheta demonstrates the flexibility of the romantic story: an alien, impoverished child learns maturity through cruel lessons till she obtains not only social acceptance, but emotional and intellectual satisfaction. She is implicitly feminist in claiming, like the Brontës, that this is the right of all women.

Emecheta's novels impart a sense of indestructible vitality in women, in spite of harrowing setbacks. Emecheta also bears witness to the social curbs on a group of women numerically in the majority, yet seldom heard: the working-class. Though middle-class in Nigeria, here her large family and low income forced her to share for a time the bad housing of social class five. *In The Ditch* is the client's view of well-meaning but insensitive social workers, classing a woman as a 'problem' because she has five children yet wishes to study.

The young English working-class novelist Pat Barker also concerns herself with women who are not seen as individuals in their own right. She points out that working-class women perform jobs like cleaning and are not meant to be seen. Most working-class male writers deal harshly with women in their novels; they see them as curbing men with pregnancies, as Emecheta's husband did. Pat Barker attempts to redress the balance with a glimpse of female sharing in *Union Street*[12]. She takes the interesting structure of seven women in the same street to depict common elements in their lives. In *Blow Your House Down*[13] she examines sexual violence against women. Novels need not be outstanding aesthetically to draw attention to a social predicament, as Harriet Beecher Stowe demonstrated with *Uncle Tom's Cabin* (1852). But they can have a sensitizing role.[14]

The Joys of Motherhood

In *The Joys of Motherhood* (1979) Emecheta strives to sensitize Nigerians to the exploitation of mothers. With increased mastery of structure and irony she describes the humiliations and small joys of a poor, unappreciated Ibo mother: 'And her reward. Did she not have the greatest funeral Ibuza had ever seen?' (p 224) Significantly a West African reviewer considers this her best novel: 'It is a remarkable talent, to make ordinary events interesting, without feeling the need to distort or exaggerate.'

The opening chapter 'The Mother' begins in the 1930s with the protagonist Nnu Ego running hysterically through the streets of Lagos to commit suicide by throwing herself in the river. The action, which appears crazy to her culture, is then explained from the inside and by relating it to her social situation. Emecheta analyses the state of mind of women valued for their biology rather than their individuality.

She explains some of Nnu Ego's difficulties by referring to her independent mother; she had not offered her an easy model to follow, because she had refused to marry, but proudly bore a son – to offer to the father. The woman can deviate from tradition slightly but needs the sanctification of the father (not the mother). Emecheta interweaves proverbs to demonstrate how her characters' actions stem from long held customs. She chooses a ballad-type story, fusing both African and European forms – as in the use of proverbs. They stress elements in the ideology of motherhood which have now become established as almost immoveable conventions.

Nnu Ego is orphaned; her character then reappears as an adolescent girl lighting her father's pipe. Her very name symbolises the relationship to her father, to whom she is priceless: 'more than 20 bags of cowries'. He loves her, in his own, not very instructive, way:

Agbadi was no different from many men. He himself might take wives and then neglect them for years, apart from seeing that they each received their one yam a day; he could bring his mistresses to sleep with him right in his courtyard while his wives pined and bit their nails for a word from him. But when it came to his own daughter, she must have a man who would cherish her. (p 29)

The effect of his love is to lead Nnu Ego to despise her husband Nnaife, because he is neither a farmer nor a hunter. He works as a houseboy in the capital, emasculated by the capitalist system, 'a womanmade man'. In Lagos racism undermines relationships, due to 'shining white man's money' (p 51). Nnu Ego must both adapt to these contemporary values *and* carry out the traditional custom of producing many offspring. The husband proclaims that it is only thanks to him that she conceives, but when she loses the child, he blames her as 'mad'. She is saved from depression by her sisters and by dreams of conceiving more children, to vindicate her existence.

Nnu Ego produces a son, but at the worst time: her husband has lost his job; the family has to live on the little she earns from trading. Yet virtue is linked to the ability to conceive and she comforts herself with the thought that the son will support her in her old age. It is motherhood, not sexual intercourse, which constitutes marriage – a sterile wife can be returned to her parents. Emecheta underlines the rigidity of the code which decrees motherhood, the *necessary state for being considered as a woman*, because Nnaife soon takes a second wife. She feels relegated to 'bowing to this perfect creature – she who had once been acclaimed the most beautiful ... Why had she become so haggard, so rough, so worn?' (p 118) When she and the second wife cannot feed their children on the little money from Nnaife, Nnu Ego realises that she is 'a prisoner, imprisoned by love for her children' (p 137). Her hopes for an honourable place in society, her investment in the future, merely serve to imprison her.

The bitter irony of her situation is emphasised in the ending: she dies alone 'with no child to hold her hand and no friend to talk to'. Neighbours agree that she had given to her children because 'the joy of being a mother was the joy of giving all to her children' (p 224). After her lonely death the successful children return, to give her a magnificent funeral.

In her treatment of the double social standards for motherhood, Emecheta can be compared to Afro-American writers, though her protagonist is even lonelier. She had no time for friendship, 'too busy building up her joys as a mother' (p 224), and it is she, not her husband, who is blamed when the children leave home. The difference lies in the fact that though they all start as victims, American heroines have the chance, however painful, of sloughing off 'the victim role to reveal the true powerful and heroic identity'.[15] In contrast, Nnu cannot articulate her victimisation. As she cannot find a language nor a group of women to help explore her seeming worthlessness, she is destroyed.

The use of proverbs, imposed on all, without taking individuality into account, emphasise the oral transmitting of values, which imprison Nnu Ego in societal concepts. She possesses no language to struggle against the weight of religion, myth, habit, culture, economics and patriarchy. Emecheta, like Alice Walker, praises the value of mothers in societies which still undervalue, underestimate and underpay them.

Destination Biafra

She approaches a vast theme in her next novel: *Destination Biafra* (1982) takes on board the appalling suffering of her Ibo people in the late 1960s. Her heroine, Debbie, is what Emecheta hopes the new African woman will be. 'She's a symbol of the new Nigerian woman, able to fly, able to handle arms.'[16] Emecheta realises the importance of giving women a new image to which they – and their menfolk – may adapt. Debbie is bright and well-educated. 'She's also a symbol of Africa, which has just been used as a means of selling arms.'[17] Although partially symbolic, the character of Debbie is well drawn and skilfully used to impart the suffering of the Ibo women and children. The wide political background is shrewdly analysed, demonstrating Emecheta's ability to learn fast. Her acceptance as a writer has given her the confidence to tackle subjects hitherto considered suitable for men.

Double Yoke

In *Double Yoke* (1982) Emecheta deals with the problems of contemporary Nigeria. Her straightforward realism is a useful vehicle for an increasingly didactic purpose: to aid the adaptation of young Nigerian students, removed from firm village values, to Western-style individualism. Her central male student Ete Kamba symbolises the dual wish to study for its own sake and to help his family. He falls in love with an apparently simple, quiet girl Nko, from a nearby village. Once they are both at university the conflict between female and male stereotypes divides them. He wants a virgin, though he has deflowered her. She is forced into sex by her professor, in order to get her degree; she also has to support her family. Like Ete Kamba, she is presented simplistically, to suggest the predicament of many modern, educated African girls.

The background characters do not live, their words function as messages. This is not a serious drawback, since the central couple is sympathetically drawn, and is contrasted with caricatures of two successful Nigerians: the Professor, also a religious leader and his sister, Mrs Dr Edet. She is too tall and successful for a woman, so constantly claims 'I'm not the pushful type'. Such irony is necessary to social satire. Emecheta combines it with farce to parody the Professor's revivalist prayer meeting and its effect on ingenuous students:

> The Reverend Professor worked himself up, swinging the microphone in the air, bellowing into it, then collecting his dumpy body and jumping up and down in religious ecstasy, the jacket of his three-piece suit flapping up and down like angry elephant's ears … as for the students, they were doing most of the crying. The music man was droning the drum, one beat at long intervals, and the Reverend Professor was saying in a low menacing voice 'yeah, confess; yeah, confess'. (p 83)

The language has Dickensian verve here; Emecheta intersperses personal comments that have the unpolished directness of speech with the African tradition of oral story-telling:

> African professors had to maintain an artificial mystified air … it was part of their survival armour. If they allowed themselves to become like other people, people would realise that they did not know that much. But Professor Ikot of the Cultural was not frightened of looking common because he claimed that it was God working through him. (p 11)

The plotting is skilful. The chapters switch from the perceptions and suffering of Ete Kamba to those of Nko. They both want too much: the qualities of tradition and the advantages of freedom. There are various clever twists at the end, including the fact that we have been reading Ete Kamba's manuscript. Emecheta brings herself in at the beginning as Creative Writing lecturer. She teaches 'that oneself was always a very good point to start writing about'. She reappears at the end, almost a 'deus ex machina' to urge her male students to bear 'your double burdens heroically' – the double burden of individualism and traditional values.

This symbol is slightly overworked, but functional. Nko's mother says 'I did not have to look for a husband. Now you have this new thing, this mad education for women, and yet still you want to have everything we had ... you are under a double yoke.' (p 94) Though Emecheta's feminism is becoming more overt, she evidences compassion for male problems. They are like Victorians in being brought up to expect submissiveness from their women folk, while the outside world suddenly imposes conflicting ideals. Thus one could claim that her Victorian-type preaching has its place.

She has widened her social framework to include criticism of corruption in modern Nigeria, where the few rich live remarkably well, and the many poor have to count their few coins. Her latest novel *The Rape of Shavi* (1983) is even more ambitious, set in the post-nuclear future. A quiet African country is invaded by whites fleeing from their own destroyed civilisation: 'It's about a culture that's been raped. At the beginning we find a group of people living a quiet, simple life. Unfortunately some whites, running away from their over-civilised culture, brought their trouble with them ... As it's the future I just use ideas.'*

At the end of the novel the king looks back over the appalling happenings and concludes: 'We have a great deal to give, we showed the Albinos how to look after each other, how to be responsible for each other. We should go on living as we used to, surviving our droughts ... .' (p 177)

Compared to Nadine Gordimer's glimpse of the future in *July's People* (1981) this is unsubtle thematically and linguistically, though it displays the conciseness and strength of fable. Gordimer imagines the probable scenario of a successful black uprising in South Africa: a white couple flee with their black servant, July, who had worked for them for fifteen years. Once they owe their survival to him, their relationships change not only with him but with each other. Gordimer stresses what Emecheta just glimpses: the capacity of political structures to change private relationships, recounted in an exciting style enriched by stream-of-consciousness.

What Emecheta has restored to the novel is the freshness of story-telling, in danger of being underestimated, even excluded by some experimentalists. Emecheta foregrounds what the *nouveau roman* disregarded, by using features of the tale from *both* European and African cultures.

Conclusion

Emecheta uses documentary, representing both Ibo and black immigrant experience in general. Severed from her culture in adolescence, she has lost its love of fabulation and fantasy, unlike her American sisters. What she shares with them is a sense of social responsibility, using the novel to explore the behaviour and values of her group – as women writers have done since the eighteenth century. When the Industrial Revolution began the middle class had no art forms to suggest how they should behave, whereas labourers had their songs and village customs, aristocrats had painting and poetry. Until recently blacks had a unique healing art-form in their music, but it is no longer exclusively theirs. The novel now performs the function of recording their unique experience, and revaluing it. 'The novel is needed now by Afro-Americans in a way it was not needed before. It should have something in it that enlightens; something in it that opens the door and points the way.'[18]

Emecheta points the way – by representing the experience of black mothers in contemporary Britain. She, together with an increasing band of sisters, have taken account of the need to interpret their community to themselves and to the alienating white power group. Emecheta exploits autobiography to look at institutionalised, cultural oppression.

Fiction can prove vital in giving us images about how we are, and how we wish to be. *Uncle Tom's Cabin* by Harriet Beecher Stowe, though flawed, achieved more than propaganda in depicting blacks as loving and loyal. Books are potent, they remain on our shelves, in libraries, in print, relaying stories about society. Emecheta offers stories of immigrant experience, a record of the effects of marginalisation, and a woman's triumph over oppression.

Notes

1 S. Namjoshi, *Feminist Fables*, Sheba, 1981, p 1.
2 Asian Women Writers' Workshop, *Right of Way*, Women's Press, 1988. See also the anthology *Charting the Journey*, Sheba, 1988.
3 A. Walker, *In Search of Our Mothers' Gardens*, Women's Press, 1984, p 69.
4 *In Search of Our Mothers' Gardens*, p 70.
5 Talk given in Camden Library, June 1986.
6 *Women: A World Report*, Methuen and New Internationalist Publications, 1985.

7   *Women: A World Report*, p 19.

8   *A Room of One's Own*, BBC Radio 4, 27 May 1984.

9   *A Room of One's Own*.

10 E. Benveniste, *Problems in General Linguistics*, Miami: University of Miami Press, 1971.

11 Fabulation implies enjoyment of fabulous stories, of fables and fantasy.

12 P. Barker, *Union Street*, Virago, 1982.

13 P. Barker, *Blow Your House Down*, Virago, 1984.

14 See J.P. Tompkins, 'Sentimental Power: Uncle Tom's Cabin and the Politics of Literary History' in *New Feminist Criticism*, ed Showalter, Virago, 1987, p 81.

15 C. Pearson and K. Pope, *The Female Hero in American and British Literature*, New York: R.R. Booker, 1981, p 13.

16 *A Room of One's Own*.

17 *A Room of One's Own*.

18 M. Evans ed, *Black Women Writers*, Pluto, 1985, pp 340–1.

This passage was given to me by the Afro-Caribbean Language and Literacy Unit of the Inner London Education Authority. It demonstrates the use made by a class of Emecheta's short story about polygamy, *A Man Needs Many Wives*:

'This story stimulated a lively discussion on polygamy. It told of a one-to-one marriage, of how the husband's brother died, which meant one of his wives had to live with the husband and wife. It described the wife's difficult and painful feelings.

The talk was again about customs and survival of the family and the effects of poverty on the customs and traditions. We talked of how the customs were being adapted, so that, for example, if a husband's brother died, the wife or wives might come and live with the other family. The husband wouldn't take on the dead brother's wife as his own but would shelter her. She and her children would be looked after and she would be encouraged to find a boyfriend, though not have children by him.

The students found the custom of polygamy totally unacceptable and felt it was all done for the man's benefit. The teacher may put some emphasis on the value of tradition in its own context and show that there were reasons for its existence.'

Useful Terminology

The words listed here may be useful in understanding both this book and those recommended in the bibliography.

ANDROGYNY – possessing female *and* male characteristics.
AUTHORIAL SELF – the writer, or author, as *narrator*, storyteller, rather than her (or him) self.
DECONSTRUCTION – a radical critique of Western thinking, initiated by Derrida, because meaning and truth were too fixed in time (and space). He considers deconstruction a 'strategy within philosophy' to displace philosophic hierarchies and closures. One of his strategies is to deconstruct concepts in Western thought based on oppositions such as dark/light, active/passive, male/female, mad/sane, which exclude the sharing of these attributes. Deconstructing such polarities opens them to new meanings and allows us to explore and redefine maleness, madness, etc.
DISCOURSE – a stretch of language longer than a sentence (in linguistics). A type of language which needs to be understood in relation to its own conventions, such as a church, a politburo pronouncement or a television chat show. We are already modifying patriarchal discourse by saying 'human being' instead of the exclusive 'Man' etc.
FABULATION – concern with fantasy and form in fiction, ideas and ideals rather than things. See Robert Scholes *Fabulation* (1967).
GENDER – aspects which are changeable; socially constructed male-femaleness as opposed to biological male-femaleness which is called SEX.
IDEOLOGY – the sum of ways we both live and represent to ourselves our relationship to conditions of existence. Ideology is inscribed in discourses, myths, presentations of 'how things are'. It offers only partial, selective, sometimes contradictory knowledge. Because it is a characteristic of language to be overlooked, the difference it constructs may seem to be natural, universal and unchangeable, whereas they are produced by a specific form of social organisation – which can be modified. Literature represents

the myths and imaginary versions of real social relationships which constitute ideology. The innovative thinking is Althusser's: 'What is represented in ideology is not the system of real relations which govern the existence of individuals, but the *imaginary*.'

IMPRESSIONISM – conveys the author's state of mind, impression or mood rather than external or objective description (as in Virginia Woolf).

INTERTEXTUALITY – the reader's experience of other texts. Intertextual elements are the recognition of similarities and differences between a text and all other texts we have read. Most novels are intertextual constructs, products of various cultural discourses on which the writing relies for intelligibility and thus needs a reader as interpreter.

LANGUE – Saussure's term for written language that makes possible our speech acts (parole).

MODERNISM – international reaction in fiction, poetry, drama and music against realism. It stresses the aesthetic, formal, mythic and symbolist. In the English-language novel it denotes writers like Joyce and Woolf, less interested in detailed description than in states of mind, experiments with language and fragmentation of form.

NATURALISM – novel writing based on extensive research into social conditions and their effect on the individual. The leading exponent is Zola, influenced by Darwin's evolutionary explanation of life.

NOUVEAU ROMAN – French novel concentrating on exploration of the world of objects rather than 'character', as in Robbe-Grillet's *La Jalousie*.

OMNISCIENT NARRATOR – author who narrates as if he or she knows everything about the characters, as in some nineteenth century novels.

POST STRUCTURALISM – developments in philosophy and criticism since Barthes. The technique used is termed deconstruction.

REIFICATION – treating a person or an idea as a thing.

REGISTER – tone of voice; a kind of writing, a style or discourse.

SEMIOLOGY – science of signs based on the work of the linguist Saussure. As developed by Lacan it is useful in film and literary criticism.

SIGN – unit of language consisting of a signifier (often a word) and a signified (idea) linked arbitrarily, not necessarily together.

STEREOTYPE – oversimplified mental representation of category of person.

STRUCTURALISM – analysis and understanding of culture as a

system of signs, where language is often used as a model. Systematic inventories of elements and their possibilities to account for meaning in literature.

SUB-TEXT – what is inferred underneath the obvious statements.

SURREALISM – a movement in the Arts, initiated in France in the 1920s. It emphasised the importance of the subconscious, and dream, based on the view that there is no right or reasonable view of the world which should dominate over what is underneath, and vital.

Basic Features of Structuralist Semiotics*

1 Language is a *sign-system* – a system of conventions for representing reality.
2 Thus, reality is always 'socially constructed' through language.
3 There is no one 'true' construction/representation of an event – only a number of culturally specific ones. There are no 'transparent', neutral accounts of the world. Structuralist semiotics opposes *empiricism*.
4 However, representations tend to present themselves *as if* they are the one possible, 'neutral', representation of an event, *the* truth.
5 Semiotics is thus concerned with (a) showing that what appears as 'natural' is in fact cultural, exposing the 'arbitrariness' (that is, the cultural specificity) of any representation and (b) exposing *which* cultural codes and conventions are at play in constructing this representation.
6 As statements are produced out of a system of conventions/codes, they depend on an audience having *learnt* these codes. This means that the media, for example, can no longer be seen as the direct conveyance of a *message* from a producer to a receiver. Rather, media 'texts' are *codified* representations, and so have to be *decoded*.
7 These codes which we have to learn have social and cultural assumptions built into them. We acquire our consciousness through learning these codes. Thus our language constitutes our consciousness, rather than us having ideas first and then *using* language to convey them. On the contrary, language uses *us*. Semiotics thus opposes *humanism*.

* With thanks to G. Diggines M.A.

8   Language works as a system of differences. Terms get their significance by being *marked off* from other terms. 'Terrorist' gets its precise meaning be being distinguished *from* 'soldier', 'guerilla', 'freedom fighter', 'volunteer', 'gunman' etc.

   Which term is *selected* from the paradigm of *possible* terms is thus crucial. Semiotics examines the implications of each such selection.

9   It also examines how each selected element (signifier) is *combined* into a *structure*. The basic premise of structuralism is that elements do not get their significance one at a time, but from the place they occupy within a structure. A term gets its precise meaning (signified) not from some abstract dictionary definition but in relation to the other terms it is combined with in the precise context, for example, the full sense of Annie Walker's 'respectability' is only produced in opposition to the 'commonness' of Hilda Ogden. The meaning of each element in a text can only be fully understood in terms of its place within the whole structure.

   This is the central methodology of structuralism – the analysis of the *internal relations* of a text.

Bibliography

Please note: all publishers are located in London, unless otherwise indicated.

Individual Bibliographies

Maya Angelou
Autobiography
I Know Why the Caged Bird Sings, Virago, 1984.
Gather Together in My Name, Virago, 1985.
Singin' and Swingin' and Getting Merry like Christmas, Virago, 1985.
And Still I Rise, Virago, 1986.
The Heart of a Woman, Virago, 1986.
Poetry
Just Give Me a Cool Drink of Water 'Fore I Diiie, New York: Random House 1971; Virago, 1988.

Angela Carter
Novels
Shadow Dance, Heinemann, 1966; as *Honeybuzzard*, New York: Simon and Schuster, 1967.
The Magic Toyshop, Heinemann, 1967; New York: Simon and Schuster, 1968.
Several Perceptions, Heinemann, 1968; New York: Simon and Schuster, 1969.
Heroes and Villains, Heinemann, 1969; New York: Simon and Schuster, 1970.
Love, Hart Davis, 1971.
The Infernal Desire Machines of Dr. Hoffman, Hart Davis, 1972; as *The War of Dreams*, New York: Harcourt Brace, 1974.
The Passion of New Eve, Gollancz, and New York: Harcourt Brace, 1977.
Nights at the Circus, Chatto and Windus, 1984.
Short Stories
Fireworks: Nine Profane Pieces, Quartet, 1974; New York: Harper and Row, 1980.
The Bloody Chamber and Other Stories, Gollancz, 1979; New York: Harper and Row, 1981.
Black Venus, Chatto and Windus, 1985.
Radio Plays
Vampirella, 1976.

138

Come unto These Yellow Sands, 1979.
The Company of Wolves, from her own story, 1980.
Poetry
Unicorn, Leeds: Location Press, 1966.
Other
Miss Z, The Dark Young Lady (juvenile), Heinemann, and New York: Simon and Schuster, 1970.
The Donkey Prince (juvenile), New York: Simon and Schuster, 1970.
Comic and Curious Cats, illustrated by Martin Leman, Gollancz, and New York: Crown, 1979.
The Sadeian Woman: An Exercise in Cultural History, Virago, 1979; as *The Sadeian Woman and the Ideology of Pornography*, New York: Pantheon, 1979.
Wayward Girls and Wicked Women (ed), Virago, 1986.
The Fairy Tales of Charles Perrault (trans), Gollancz, 1977; New York: Avon, 1978.

Buchi Emecheta
In the Ditch, Allison and Busby, 1972.
Second-Class Citizen, Allison and Busby, 1974.
The Bride Price, Allison and Busby, 1976.
The Slave Girl, Allison and Busby, 1977.
The Joys of Motherhood, Allison and Busby, 1979.
Destination Biafra, Allison and Busby, 1982.
Naira Power and *Double Yoke*, Ogwugwu Afor, 1982.
The Rape of Shavi, Ogwugwu Afor, 1983.
Head Above Water, Fontana, 1986.
She has also written children's books and television plays. Ogwugwu Afor is Emecheta's own publishing firm.

Elaine Feinstein
The Circle, Hutchinson, 1970.
Selected Poems of Marina Tsvetayeva, Hutchinson, 1971.
The Amberstone Exit, Hutchinson, 1972.
The Celebrants and Other Poems, Hutchinson, 1973.
Children of the Rose and *The Ecstasy of Dr Miriam*, Hutchinson, 1976.
Some Unease and Angels, Hutchinson, 1977.
The Shadow Master, Hutchinson, 1978.
Feast of Euridice, Hutchinson, 1980.
The Survivors, Hutchinson, 1982.
The Border, Hutchinson, 1984.
Bessie Smith, Penguin, 1986. A biography.
Marina Tsvetayeva, Penguin, 1987. A biography.
Mother's Girl, Hutchinson, 1988.

Toni Morrison

The Bluest Eye, New York: Holt Rinehart, 1970; Chatto and Windus, 1980.
Sula, Allen Lane, and New York: Knopf, 1974.
Song of Solomon, New York: Knopf, 1977; Chatto and Windus, 1978.
Tar Baby, Chatto and Windus, and New York: Knopf, 1981.
Beloved, Chatto and Windus, 1987.

Grace Nichols

i is a long memoried woman, Women's Press, 1983.
The Fat Black Woman's Poems, Sheba, 1984.
Whole of a Morning Sky, Sheba, 1986.
Lazy Thoughts of a Lazy Woman, Virago, 1990.

Olive Senior

Talking of Trees, Jamaica: Calabash, 1985.
Summer Lightning, Jamaica: Calabash, 1987; Heinemann, 1988.

Jean Rhys 1894–1979

The Left Bank (stories), Jonathan Cape, 1927.
Postures, Chatto and Windus, 1928; New York: Simon and Schuster, 1929; as
    Quartet, Andre Deutsch, 1969; New York: Harper and Row, 1971.
After Leaving Mr Mackenzie, Jonathan Cape, 1930; Alfred Knopf, 1931; Andre
    Deutsch, 1969; New York: Harper and Row, 1972.
Voyage in the Dark, Constable, 1934; New York: William Morrow, 1935;
    Andre Deutsch, 1967; New York: William Norton, 1968.
Good Morning Midnight, Constable, 1939; Andre Deutsch, 1967; New York:
    Harper and Row, 1970.
Wide Sargasso Sea, Andre Deutsch, 1966; New York: William Norton, 1967.
Tigers are Better Looking, Andre Deutsch, 1968; New York: Harper and Row,
    1974.
I Spy a Stranger and *Temps Perdu*, Penguin Modern Stories, 1969.
Sleep if Off, Lady, Andre Deutsch, 1976; New York: Harper and Row, 1976.
Smile, Please, Andre Deutsch, 1979; New York: Harper and Row, 1979.
Letters 1931–1966, Andre Deutsch, 1984.

Alice Walker

The Third Life of Grange Copeland, New York: Harcourt Brace Jovanovich,
    1970; Women's Press, 1985.
Meridian, New York: Harcourt Brace, 1976.
You Can't Keep a Good Woman Down, New York: Harcourt Brace, 1981;
    Women's Press, 1982.
The Color Purple, New York: Harcourt Brace, 1982; Women's Press, 1983.
In Love and Trouble: Stories of Black Women, Women's Press, 1984.
In Search of Our Mothers' Gardens, New York: Harcourt Brace, 1983;
    Women's Press, 1984.

Once, Women's Press, 1986.

Horses Make a Landscape Look More Beautiful, New York: Harcourt Brace, 1984; Women's Press, 1985.

Revolutionary Petunias and Other Poems, Women's Press, 1986.

Good Night, Willie Lee, I'll See You in the Morning, Women's Press, 1987.

Living by the Word: Selected Writings 1973–1987, Women's Press, 1988.

The Temple of My Familiar, Women's Press, 1989.

Zora Neale Hurston, *I Love Myself, Reader* (ed), Virago, 1985.

Useful General Criticism

Bradbury, M., ed, *Possibilities: Essays on the State of the Novel*, Oxford University Press, 1973.

The Novel Today, ed, Fontana, 1977. This contains Murdoch 'Against Dryness' and Lodge 'The Novelist at the Crossroads'.

The Contemporary English Novel, Arnold, 1979. This includes Byatt 'People in Paper Houses' and Sage 'Female Fiction'.

Burgess, A., *The Novel Now*, Faber, 1967. Burgess is wide-ranging and idiosyncratic, with a perceptive chapter on women.

Enright, D.J., *A Mania for Words*, Oxford University Press, 1984. Enright takes a traditional approach. He includes a short article on Lady Murosaka's 11th Century *The Tale of Genji*.

Hardy, B., *The Appropriate Form*, Athlone Press, 1964.

Tellers and Listeners, Athlone Press, 1975. Perceptive writing from a woman critic who was Leavisite, but who appreciates aspects of modern theory.

Jackson, R., *Fantasy*, Methuen, 1983. She uses new criticism incisively.

Josipovici, G., *The World and the Book*, Macmillan, 1971. Josipovici introduces French criticism (especially Barthes), imaginatively, with essays on Proust, Dante and the rise of the novel.

Lodge, D., *The Language of Fiction*, Routledge and Kegan Paul, 1980. Adapts modern criticism.

Working with Structuralism, Routledge and Kegan Paul, 1981. Lodge does not provide a thorough introduction, but he approaches the topic for a beginner.

Ong, W., *Orality and Literacy*, Methuen, 1982. Ong presents an imaginative, erudite study of the oral traditions of the working-class and women.

Rawling, C., ed, *Popular Fiction and Social Change*, Macmillan, 1984. Contains a seminal article on science fiction by M. Jordin.

Sartre, J.P., *What is Literature*, New York: Harper Colophon, 1965. Worth re-reading.

Tanner, T., *City of Words: American Fiction 1950–70*, Cape, 1971. Tanner states that 'a novel should be able to contain in language our destiny.'

Wilson, A., *Diversity and Depth*, Secker and Warburg, 1984. Angus Wilson has collected a good range of his reviews, on *Clarissa*, Camus, Murdoch, Claude Simon and many others.

A useful reference work is *Contemporary Novelists*, New York: St Martins Press, 1982. It offers brief accounts of the novels and bibliographies, as does *The Oxford Companion to English Literature*, ed Margaret Drabble, Oxford University Press, 1985.

Contemporary Criticism

Barthes, Roland, *Mythologies*, Cape, 1972. These fascinating, concise, approachable essays use his sign-system to analyse myths, books, even wrestling. Read *S/Z*, Cape, 1975, for his analysis of Balzac's realism.
A Barthes Reader, ed, Susan Sontag, Cape, 1985. Provides a brilliant, idiosyncratic introduction, putting him in an older French tradition.

Belsey, Catherine, *Critical Practice*, Methuen, 1980. This text provides the best written brief introduction to the theories of Barthes and Derrida.

Bergonzi, Bernard, *The Myth of Modernism and Twentieth Century Literature*, Harvester, 1985. He relates literature to its cultural context.

Culler, Jonathan, *On Deconstruction: Theory and Criticism after Structuralism*, Ithaca, New York: Cornell University Press, 1982. Culler is erudite and helpful.

Derrida, Jacques, *Writing and Difference*, Chicago: University of Chicago Press, 1975.

Eagleton, Terry, *Myths of Power, a Marxist Study of the Brontës*, Macmillan, 1975. This offers a perceptive introduction to Marxist criticism. Then read his thorough *Marxism and Literary Theory*, Methuen, 1976. One of the most reliable introductions to recent theory is his paperback *Literary Theory*, Oxford: Blackwell, 1983. Eagleton is a major contemporary critic.

Hawkes, Terence, *Structuralism and Semiotics*, Methuen, 1977. Hawkes offers a historical introduction, clear exposition and an annotated bibliography.

Kearney, Richard, *The Wake of the Imagination (Ideas of Creativity in Western Culture)*, Hutchinson, 1987. This Irish philosopher writes on modern French theory enthusiastically. He points out that postmodernism need not relinquish all humanism if it respects the ethical imagination.

Macherey, Pierre, *A Theory of Literary Production*, Routledge and Kegan Paul, 1978. This is a demanding text by a leading Marxist.

Punter, David, *The Hidden Script: Writing and the Unconscious*, Routledge, 1985. Punter offers an illuminating, uneven investigation of the unconscious in Carter, Lessing, Bainbridge, Ballard and others.

Selden, Raman, *A Reader's Guide to Contemporary Literary Theory*, Sussex: Harvester, 1980. Professor Selden expounds theory from Bakhtin and Lukacs to Foucault and Kristeva, with guides to further reading.

Feminist Literary Criticism

The most helpful introductions are:

Greene and Kahn, eds, *Making a Difference*, Methuen, 1985. This collection includes essays on varieties of feminist criticism, American, French, black and lesbian criticism.

Humm, Maggie, *Feminist Criticism: Women as Contemporary Writers*, Harvester, 1986. Humm explores contemporary theory and its effect on women writers.

Moi, Toril, *Sexual/Textual Politics*, Methuen, 1985. Moi gives the clear, forceful theoretical underpinning she claims feminist criticism needs. She has written the clearest explanation of *French Feminist Thought*, Oxford: Blackwell, 1987.

For extracts of French feminist texts see Marks and de Courtivron, eds, *New French Feminisms*, Sussex: Harvester, 1981.

Elaine Showalter, ed, *The New Feminist Criticism*, Virago, 1986. Professor Showalter includes many pathbreaking recent articles.

Re-reading Patriarchy

Figes, Eva, *Patriarchal Attitudes*, Macmillan, 1970.

Greer, Germaine, *The Female Eunuch*, MacGibbon and Kee, 1970. Greer is still powerful.

Millett, Kate, *Sexual Politics*, Virago, 1977. Millett packs her punches.

Reading/Writing like a Woman

These texts are listed chronologically, as there is a progression in the approach to 'Images of Women' in Anglo-American criticism.

Spacks, Patricia Meyer, *The Female Imagination*, Allen and Unwin, 1976. Spacks bases her articles on perceptive discussions with students about this vast and problematic topic. Today she is criticised for revealing a white middle-class bias, but she is worth reading on the nineteenth century.

Moers, Ellen, *Literary Women: The Great Writers*, New York: Doubleday, 1976; Women's Press, 1977. Moers surveys nineteenth-century novelists, brilliantly.

Showalter, Elaine, *A Literature of Their Own: British Women Novelists from Bronte to Lessing*, Princeton, New Jersey: Princeton University Press, 1977; Virago, 1978. Epochmaking.

Fetterley, Judith, *The Resisting Reader: Feminist Approaches to American Fiction*, Indiana: Indiana University Press, 1978. This is a valuable re-reading.

Gilbert, Sandra M., and Gubar, Susan, *The Madwoman in the Attic: The Woman Writer and the Nineteenth Century Literary Imagination*, New York: Yale University Press, 1979. This is an exciting study which concentrates on the psychology of women writers and heroines.

Jacobus, Mary, ed, *Women Writing and Writing about Women*, Croom Helm, 1979.

Kolodny, Annette, 'Dancing Through the Minefield' in *Feminist Studies*, 6: 1, pp 1–25.

Abel, Elizabeth, ed, *Writing and Sexual Difference*, Sussex: Harvester, 1982. Abel includes some illuminating but demanding theorists.

Beauman, Nicola, *A Very Great Profession*, Virago, 1983.

Roe, S., ed, *Women Reading Women's Writing*, Sussex: Harvester, 1987.

Deconstructing Gender

Jardine, Lisa, *Still Harping on Daughters: Women and Drama in the Age of Shakespeare*, Sussex: Harvester, 1983. Enlightening use of feminist approaches.

Keohane, Rosaldo and Gelpi, *Feminist Theory*, Sussex: Harvester, 1982. These three editors introduce invaluable articles, including Myra Jehlen 'Archimedes and the Paradox of Feminist Criticism' which opens: 'Feminist thinking is really *rethinking*', pp 189–194.

Kristeva, Julia, *Desire in Language: A Semiotic Approach to Literature and Art*, France: Roudiez, 1980; Oxford: Blackwell, and New York: Simon and Schuster, 1981. Difficult yet worthwhile.

Marks, Elaine and de Courtivron, Isabelle (eds), *New French Feminisms: An Anthology*, Sussex: Harvester, 1981. This offers helpful translations from a wide selection of texts, difficult to obtain elsewhere, including essays by Luce Irigaray and Hélène Cixous.

Wandor, Michelene, *On Gender and Writing*, Pandora, 1983. This book consists of useful interviews with a wide range of women writers and feminists.

Women Writing about Women Writing

Baym, Nina, *Women's Fiction*, Ithaca, New York: Cornell University Press, 1978. Baym's thesis is that pious heroines represent moral strength and domesticity equals pragmatic feminism.

Beauman, Nicola, *A Very Great Profession: The Women's Novel 1914–1939*, Virago, 1983. A superficial survey of the plots of many women's novels.

Ellman, Mary, *Thinking about Women*, Virago, 1979.

Evans, Mari, ed, *Black Woman Writers 1950–1980*, New York: Anchor Press, 1984; Pluto Press, 1985. Evans presents a wonderful selection of interviews with major black writers and articles on their work.

Figes, Eva, *Sex and Subterfuge*, Macmillan, 1983. Figes analyses similarities of structure in eighteenth century English novelists, in a social context.

Hardwick, Elizabeth, *Seduction and Betrayal*, Weidenfeld and Nicholson, 1970. Hardwick's essays are readable, thought provoking and brief.

Olsen, Tillie, *Silences*, New York: Delacorte, 1965; Virago, 1980. Tillie Olsen offers a poet's view of difficulties in writing and publishing.

Rich, Adrienne, *On Lies, Secrets and Silence: Selected Prose 1966–78*, New

York: W. W. Norton, 1979; Virago, 1980. This is a major book by a leading lesbian poet and thinker.

Stubbs, Patricia, *Women and Fiction: Feminism and the American Novel 1880–1920*, Sussex: Harvester, 1979. This is an uneven but useful study.

Zeman, Anthea, *Presumptuous Girls: Women and Their World in the Serious Woman's Novel*, Weidenfeld and Nicholson, 1977. Zeman's title promises more than it gives, but covers interesting English novelists.

Black Feminist Literary Criticism

Christian, B., *Black Feminist Criticism*, New York: Athene, 1988.

Cobham, R. and Collins, M., eds, *Watchers and Seekers*, Women's Press, 1987.

Da Choong, *Black Women Talk Poetry*, Blackwomen Talk, 1989.

Dabydeen, D., ed, *The Black Presence in English Literature*, Manchester: Manchester University Press, 1985.

Evans, M., ed, *Black Women Writers*, New York: Anchor, 1984; Pluto, 1985. Wide-ranging, with articles by the writers and about them.

McDowell, D., 'New Directions for Black Feminist Criticism' in *New Feminist Criticism*, ed Showalter, Virago, 1986. A pathbreaking article.

Grewal, S., ed, *Charting the Journey*, Sheba Press, 1988.

Ngcobo, L., *Let It Be Told: Black Women Writers in Britain*, Pluto, 1987.

Scafe, Suzanne, *Teaching Black Literature*, Virago, 1989.

Schipper, M., ed, *Unheard Words: Women and Literature in Africa, the Arab World, Asia, the Caribbean and Latin America*, Allison and Busby, 1985. A helpful, though slightly superficial introduction. Interesting features are the inclusion of interviews and proverbs from each section of the globe.

Smith, B., 'Towards a Black Feminist Criticism' in *New Feminist Criticism*, ed Showalter, Virago, 1986. Another pathbreaking article.

Tate, C., *Black Writers at Work*, Harpenden, Herts: Oldcastle Books, 1985.

Washington, M.H., *Invented Lives: Narratives of Black Women 1860–1960*, New York: Anchor Press, 1987.

Willis, S., 'Black Women Writers' in *Making a Difference*, eds Greene and Kahn, Methuen, 1985.

Feminism

Barrett, Michele, *Women's Oppression Today*, Verso, 1980, provides a forceful introductory account.

Brunt, Rosalind and Rowan, Caroline, *Feminism, Culture and Politics*, Lawrence and Wishart, 1982. They present an exceedingly useful range of essays, including Barrett 'A Definition of Cultural Politics'.

Cameron, Deborah, *Feminism and Linguistic Theory*, Macmillan, 1985. The clearest comprehensive survey of the strengths (and weaknesses) of present theoretical positions, written with common sense and revolutionary vision.

Eisenstein, Hester, *Contemporary Feminist Thought*, Unwin, 1985. A wide-ranging account of differing historical, social and literary attitudes.

Feminist Review contains many relevant articles. It is published three times a year by a collective, 65, Manor Road, London N.16.

Heilbrun, Carolyn, *Toward a Recognition of Androgyny*, New York: Harper Colophon Books, 1973. This is a valuable analysis, and a necessary adjunct to feminist enquiry.

Miller, Casey and Swift, Kate, *Words and Women*, Pelican, 1979. They present a useful analysis of discrimination in the language of educational books.

Mitchell, Juliet, *Psychoanalysis and Feminism*, Harmondsworth: Penguin, 1976. Mitchell is one of the leading British feminists to use psychoanalysis.

Oakley, Ann, *Sex, Gender and Society*, Temple Smith, 1972, offers helpful distinctions.

Radcliffe Richards, Janet, *The Sceptical Feminist*, Penguin, 1983. This presents a sensible critique of a few exaggerated claims.

Spender, Dale, writes clearly and prolifically, but untheoretically. Her epochmaking book was *Man Made Language*, Routledge and Kegan Paul, 1980. She analyses patriarchal discrimination in everyday language, with many cogent examples.

Woman of Ideas, Ark, 1985, presents summaries of often neglected women writers and thinkers from Aphra Behn to the present day.

For the Record: The Making and Meaning of Feminist Knowledge, Women's Press, 1985. Spender offers accounts of ideas from Friedan onwards.

Mothers of the Novel, Pandora, 1986. Spender describes the lives of 100 women novelists before Jane Austen, but with little analysis of their books.

Further Reading of Enjoyable Background Books

Beer, Gillian, *Romance*, Methuen, 1970. From the Middle Ages to the 1920s.

Fleenor, Juliann, *The Female Gothic*, Canada: Eden Press, 1983.

Griffiths, J., ed, *Caribbean Connections*, Commission for Racial Equality, 1984. Invaluable booklist.

Howells, C.A., *Private and Fictional Worlds: Canadian Women Novelists of the 1970s and 1980s*, Methuen, 1987. Readable introduction to Margaret Atwood, Alice Munro, Margaret Laurence, Joan Barfoot etc.

Hurston, Zora Neale, *Dust Tracks on a Road*, Virago, 1990.

Jackson, Rosemary, *Fantasy: The Literature of Subversion*, Methuen, 1983.

Kenyon, O., *Women Novelists Today*, Hemel Hempstead: Harvester, 1988.

Kirkham, Margaret, *Jane Austen, Feminism and Fiction*, Sussex: Harvester, 1983. Useful if you wish to see how a feminist re-interprets well-known novels and shows how many ideas of Mary Wollstonecraft and others appear in Austen.

Osler, Audrey, *Speaking Out: Black Girls in Britain*, Virago, 1990.

Palmer, Paulina, *Contemporary Women's Fiction: Narrative Practice and Feminist Theory*, Hemel Hempstead: Harvester, 1989. Palmer looks at less frequently read novels, including lesbian and radical feminist works.

Partnoy, Alicia, *You Can't Drown the Fire: Latin American Women Writing in Exile*, Virago, 1989. Stirring factual and fictional accounts of recent experiences.

Wilson, Amrit, *Finding A Voice*, Virago, 1988. Experiences of Asian women in Britain.

Index

Achebe, Chinua, 52, 122
Africa, 62–3, 64, 76, 77–8, 116, 117–18, 119, 129–31
African, 86–7, 90–1, 95–6, 100–101, 111, 113, 115, 118, 121, 130
Afro-American, 57, 64, 90, 117, 128
Afro-Caribbean, 52, 114, 119, 133
Akhmatova, Anna, 40, 45–7
alienation, 29, 30, 39, 65, 107, 115, 117, 132
allegory, 27, 126
American Indians, 78, 111
Angelou, Maya, 10, Chap. 4, 78, 84, 91, 117, 119, 120
archetype, 58, 90
Arnold, Matthew, 2, 10
Asian, 114
Atwood, Margaret, 9
Austen, Jane, 20

Baldwin, James, 52, 73, 109
Bambara, Toni Cade, 51, 60, 66
Beauvoir, Simone de, 24
Behn, Aphra, 1
Bellow, Saul, 32, 97
Bennett, Louise, 102
Black
  art, 55, 56, 66, 72, 96–7, 132
  women, 51–133
  literature, 53, 55, 80, 131
  Power, 52, 84
  press(es), 108, 116, 121
  sexism, 52, 57, 79, 129
  speech, 9, 51–2, 55, 70–1, 87, 94, 97, 100, 103, 108–9, 113, 117, 118, 119, 120, 124–5, 129
  creativity, see Chaps. 5–8
  worship, 57

Borges, 30
Bradbury, Malcolm, 141
Brecht, 21, 125
Brontë, Charlotte, 2, 20, 106, 126
  Jane Eyre, 3, 20, 35, 106, 126
Brontë, Emily, Wuthering Heights, 20
Burgess, Anthony, 49, 125

Cameron, Deborah, 13, 145
Caribbean, 51, 99–112, 114
Carter, Angela, 2, 6, 9, 10, 12–31, 120
Cervantes, 27
Christian, Barbara, 53, 64, 80, 89, 98, 145
Cixous, Hélène, 7, 144
Cocteau, 16
Collins, Merle, 100, 101, 107–9, 111

deconstruction, 7–8, 10, 11, 134
Derrida, 7–8, 10, 72, 134, 142
Dickens, Charles, 87, 130
difference, 6–7, 72, 110
Dostoyevsky, 32
Drabble, Margaret, 14, 124, 126, 142

Emecheta, Buchi, 9, 10, 73, 54–5, 109, 113–33
  Second-Class Citizen, 73, 115–6, 123–5
Eve, 34
  The Passion of New Eve, 17, 23–5

fabulation, 13, 31, 82, 131, 132, 134
Fairbairns, Zoë, 35
fairytale, 13, 15, 17, 18, 25, 26, 97
fantasy, 12, 15, 17, 18, 20, 26, 27, 53, 121
Feinstein, 33, 39–50
  The Border, 39, 40, 44–5

female, 8, 9, 12, 13, 16, 20, 25, 27, 40, 49, 54, 55, 64, 66, 72, 73, 76, 80, 89, 101, 108, 117, 121, 124, 129
female gothic, 19–21, 31, 146
feminine, 4, 6, 8, 10, 12, 14, 23, 30, 85
Foucault, 22
Freud, Sigmund, 3

gender, 7, 24, 33, 40, 53, 85, 134
    Look Back in Gender, 33, 49
    On Gender and Writing, 31, 33
Gilbert, S. and Gubar S., 72, 143
gothic, 2, 15, 17, 18–21, 27, 54
Gordimer, Nadine, 131
Griffiths, Joan, 112, 146

Hardwick, Elizabeth, 144
Head, Bessie, 9, 14, 109, 117, 120–1
Holocaust, 33, 39, 93
Hurston, Zora Neale, 51, 141, 146

immigrant, Chaps. 7 and 8
Irigaray Luce, 7

Jamaica(n), 105
journalism, 13, 28, 113
Joyce, James, *Ulysses*, 7, 108

Kant, 10
Kaplan, Cora, 5, 85, 98
Kinkaid, Jamaica, 104
Kolodny, A., 10, 11, 144
Kristeva, Julia, 7, 8, 11, 144

Lacan, Jacques, 6–7
Lawrence, D.H., 4
Leavis, F.R., 2, 10
lesbian, 5, 68, 75, 89
Lessing, Doris, 4, 12, 22
Lurie, Alison, 6

magic realism, 18, 82, 90
male, 1, 2, 6, 7, 8, 11, 13, 14, 16, 27, 29, 39, 42, 52, 54–5, 57–8, 66, 73, 75, 79, 84, 90, 92, 93, 101, 129
Manning, Olivia, 50

Marquez, Gabriel Garcia, 18, 86
Marx, Karl, 3
Marxist, 5, 11, 12, 27, 45, 125
Miller, Arthur, 32
Miller, Henry, 4
Millett, Kate, 4, 143
Moers, Ellen, 4, 19
Moi, Toril, 143
Morrison, Toni, 9, 10, Chaps. 4 and 8, 83–98, 100, 101, 110, 113
Murdoch, Iris, 2, 5, 6, ll, 12, 69
myth, 13, 23, 25, 26, 28, 30, 42, 45, 53, 64, 86, 87, 96, 114, 129
    de-mythologising, 13, 77
    re-mythologising, 13, 29, 30
mythology, 110–11

Namjoshi, Suniti, 114, 132
Naipaul,V.S., 102
Nietszche, 62
Nichols, Grace, 101, 110–11
Nigerian, 113–31
nouveau roman, 29, 131, 135

O'Brien, Edna, 126
O'Connor, Flannery, 88
omissions, 5

Patriarch(y)al, 1, 3, 7, 8, 9, 72, 107
Picaresque, 27
Piercy, Marge, 121
polygamy, 121, 133
Pratt, Annis, 5
Proust, Marcel, 41
psyche, 44
psychiatric, 38
psychoanalysis, 6–8
psychotherapeutic, 74, 79

Radcliffe, Anne, *The Mysteries of Udolpho*, 2, 19
Reich, W., 23
Rhys, Jean, 1, 10, 35, 101, 102, 105–8, 112
Rilke, 63
Roberts, Michèle, 35

Roe, Sue, 31, 144
romance, 15, 105, 107, 146
romantic, 1, 20, 126
romanticise, 62
rubens, Bernice, 33, 36–9, 50

de Sade, 12, 20
The Sadeian Woman, 13, 23, 24, 25
Saussure, 2, 3, 10, 135
Science fiction, 1, 15, 17, 24, 40
semiotics, 7, 8, 135, 136–7
Senior, Olive, 101–5
sexism, 52, 57, 79, 85, 127–8
sexual, 14, 23, 24, 44, 52, 53, 74, 75,
    79, 101, 104, 107, 128
sexuality, 5, 17, 23, 25, 33, 54, 65, 68,
    106, 118
Shakespeare, 91
Showalter, Elaine, 4, 143
sisterhood, 76
Smith, Barbara, 52, 53, 60, 89, 98,
    145
Solzhenitzyn, 78
Spacks, Patricia Meyer, 4, 5, 143
Spender, Dale, *Mothers of the Novel*,
    2, 105, 146

spirituality, 69, 118
stereotype, 1, 15, 16, 17, 24, 29, 69,
    129
structuralism, 2–3, 135

Todd, Janet, 60
Tsvetayeva, Marina, 40, 45–6, 50

Uncle Tom's Cabin, 127, 132, 133

Victorian, 29, 126, 131

Walker, Alice, 9, 10, 51, 61–82, 101,
    115, 116, 117, 118, 121
    The Color Purple, 3, 65, 67–72, 73,
    74–80
Walker, Margaret, 66
Wandor, M., 31, 33–6, 49, 144
Washington, Mary Helen, 66, 73, 81,
    145
Weldon, Fay, 69, 81
womanism, 67, 121
Women's Movement, 5, 14, 111, 121
Woolf, Virginia, 7
working class, 113, 114, 126–7
Wright, Richard, 52, 57, 64